DEALING WITH STRESS

Managing its Impact

DEALING WITH STRESS

Managing its Impact

Susan Leigh

Published by:
Stellar Books LLP
Dunham Gatehouse
Charcoal Road
Bowdon
Cheshire
WA14 4RY

www.stellarbooks.co.uk

ISBN: 978-1910275

Published in January 2016

www.susanleigh.net

www.lifestyletherapy.net

A catalogue record for this book is available at the British Library.

Designed and typeset in Garamond by Stellar Books

This book is dedicated to my late husband, Frederick Leigh,

without whom none of this would have happened.

And to my gorgeous boy, Tiger who has meticulously

supervised pretty much every word I've written,

snoozing across my arms as I tried to write.

Thank you.

BOOKS BY SUSAN LEIGH

Dealing with Death, Coping with the Pain

Dealing with Stress, Managing its Impact

CONTENTS

CHAPTER THREE   Stress And Relationships

CHAPTER FOUR   Stress and Friends

CHAPTER SEVEN   Stress and Health

CHAPTER EIGHT   Stress and Final Thoughts

INTRODUCTION

Dealing with Stress, Managing its Impact

S tress is a fact of life, a life that consists of good and bad experiences, occasional life or death situations and assorted pressures and mishaps. As human beings we're designed to cope with stress, handle urgent situations and then react accordingly, but once they're dealt with, it's important to allow time to recover, relax and become calm again.

It's been discovered that even babies growing in the womb are affected by any stress their host mother may be experiencing. And, after birth, as we go through our lives, the various situations we experience, the way we're treated and any patterns of behaviour we've established will all combine with our personality and DNA to colour and influence our reaction and resilience to stress.

Consequently one person's reaction to stressful situations can vary dramatically from another's and indeed we can also find that how we react to stress can vary from one day to the next. The way we're feeling, whether we've slept or not, our personal circumstances, as well as our relationship, domestic and financial situations will all have a bearing on our ability to cope with stress.

When we're overloaded and not coping well with life, stress can become a negative factor and inhibit our body from taking care of itself. It will prevent it from functioning well, from adapting, healing and repairing itself. The impact of persistent, unremitting stress can ultimately cause emotional and health-related issues.

Think about crossing a road in a leisurely fashion until you see a car racing towards you. At times like that our body automatically goes into 'fight or flight' mode. This motivates us to either run quickly out of harm's way or stay and fight, whichever is deemed the most appropriate response. But if we find ourselves in a constant state of stress our body can become conditioned to be on 'red alert' all the time.

Let's look at what happens to our body when we're in stressful situations:

When we determine a situation to be stressful our sympathetic nervous system, which is part of the autonomic nervous system, activates the 'fight or flight' response and our brain sends signals to the adrenal glands to release stress hormones such as adrenaline, cortisol and norepinephrine. This allows our body to deal with the immediate requirements for survival, to act faster and physically prepare for action.

Recall the example I used of crossing the road. As the car quickly nears us we need to react quickly, run without thinking out of harm's way. When we reach safety we may find that our heart's racing, stomach's churning, we may need to visit the bathroom as a matter of urgency, experience jelly legs, find that we're shaking or have difficulty breathing.

Our entire focus has been the immediacy of the situation. This causes the respiratory system to speed up, heart rate to increase, blood pressure to increase and liver to produce more glucose, more blood sugar for instant energy and muscle tone increase. Other body functions such as digestion, urinary and reproductive functions slow down or shut off for the duration and blood may well drain away from the skin.

Over time chronic ongoing stress slowly depletes the body's reserves and can cause complications or diseases to affect the body's systems. It can even contribute towards a heart attack or stroke. Many of the recognised 360 physical symptoms of stress are often attributed to more serious physical conditions because those responses can cause palpitations, chest pain and rapid heartbeat and gut-related problems like Irritable Bowel Syndrome or headaches.

Other symptoms can include loss of libido, food-related issues like over or under-eating, sleeping problems, low energy, greater sensitivity to aches, pains, and tense muscles, frequent colds and infections, nervousness and shaking, ringing in the ears, cold or sweaty hands and feet, excessive sweating, dry mouth and difficulty swallowing, clenched jaw and grinding teeth. It's quite a catalogue!

Sustained stress can also impact on our emotional responses to situations, causing us to become easily agitated, frustrated and moody. We may find that we feel overwhelmed, like we're losing control or feel the need to take control, have difficulty relaxing and quieting our mind, feel bad about ourselves (low self-esteem), lonely, worthless and depressed. We may even start to avoid others because of the stress it causes.

Physically, once the stress has abated:

After short periods of stress the parasympathetic nervous system tries to help us return back to normal, just as the sympathetic nervous system intervened to help us deal with the demands of the situation, to react and survive.

Once we learn to recognise our own personal warning signals of stress and appreciate that our response to stress is becoming too prolonged or intense we can start to introduce better ways to manage each situation. Introducing stress prevention and stress management techniques can help us to support better health and maintain a better quality of life for ourselves and those who are affected by our behaviour, those whom we come into contact with; family, friends, co-workers, even other road users!

How to Use This Book

This book is not intended as a substitute for counselling. There is no jargon or set of rules to follow. It's a book about helping with the difficult events that sometimes come our way in the key, important areas of our lives. Its aim is to offer alternative insights, options and perspectives to help you manage the negative feelings and reactions that you may experience at those stressful times.

It's not intended to be read straight through, from beginning to end, but rather dipped into as and when required. There may be some slight duplication of content on occasion as some stressful situations can impact on more than one area of life.

I read somewhere that it's not what happens to us in life that matters; it's how we respond and react that makes all the difference to our quality of life, health and wellbeing. This book's goal is to teach you to respond in a more appropriate and healthy way, ready and able to Live Life Well.

CHAPTER ONE

Stress and You

Do Your Words Reveal That You're Stressed?

Many of us don't fully appreciate the impact that stress has upon us, especially if it's sustained over a long period of time. We may accept that we're busy, acknowledge the many demands on our time but regard our stressed state as a normal part of modern life, of having a career, children, a business. Everyone we know is equally busy. We'll be sure to make time to relax on our next holiday!

Stress in itself can be useful. It's part of life that helps us to run faster to avoid a speeding car, deliver a pitch to an important client, be able to think outside the box. But staying in a heightened state of awareness, constantly analysing, being unable to switch off can cause our physical and mental health to suffer.

Often there are physical and verbal clues that our stress levels are escalating. We may have consulted our doctor, had tests because of the headaches, stomach problems, skin rashes, irritability, difficultly concentrating. The usual outcome is 'you're fine but need to learn how to relax'. And, as it's been documented that there are over 360 symptoms of stress, it's no wonder that stress is so evident in many areas of life, health and wellbeing.

Let's look at how your choice of words can reveal that you're stressed:

- How many of us are familiar with the phrase 'It's doing my head in'. It's often said when someone's feeling overwhelmed and unable to find a solution to a difficult problem. Tension headaches, seeing dots before the eyes, dry mouth, difficulty swallowing, or having a negative perspective on life are all clues that our stress levels are increasing.

  When overwhelmed, some people will try to 'buy' themselves extra time by missing meals or aim to boost their energy levels with sugar and caffeine in order to stay awake and cram more into each day. But this often results in adrenalin overload and disturbed sleep as they continue working until bedtime and wonder why their minds are still racing.

  Help yourself by becoming more assertive; explain your pressures to others in a confident manner and take control by maybe delegating or learning to say 'no' at times rather than a programmed, automatic 'yes'.

- When someone feels emotionally hurt, let down or disappointed it's not uncommon to hear them utter phrases like 'I'm gutted', 'I feel sick to my stomach'. Emotional stress can manifest itself through Irritable Bowel Syndrome and other gut-related conditions.

  Become familiar with the situations that cause your stomach to go 'off', your digestive problems to flare up. Then you'll be able to recognise your own warning signs and decide how best to handle them, maybe by learning to speak up, becoming more confident and assertive. Introduce better habits and intercept problems earlier, rather than allowing them to escalate and become stressful.

- Do you know someone who when they feel irritable, irritated and angry make revealing comments like 'He/it really gets under my skin'. How interesting that they then display itchy red skin, rashes, and the triggering of old skin conditions. Suggest they examine areas of irritation in their life, the things that they don't like to say or deal with. Suppressed feelings can cause associated stress to erupt through physical symptoms.

- When we're feeling stressed we may say 'I can't see straight' because our decisions and choices have become overwhelming and hazy. We may experience blurred vision, spots before the eyes, headaches. This can cause fear and reactive behaviour, panicked choices, poor decision-making in a desperate bid to deal with things quickly.

Communicating more firmly and honestly with others, asking for help, installing systems and processes, becoming effective at note-taking, using lists can all help in managing a busy life.

Support yourself by being more efficient. Introduce techniques to manage your life and the associated stresses effectively. Commit to winding down by finishing work a couple of hours before bedtime; turn off your technology, plan for exercise, healthy meals, try to go to bed a little earlier and book regular dates to have fun. If you're in a stressful phase of your life allow friends and colleagues to help. Try to share the load a little and enjoy how much more productive you become as you enjoy a better quality of life.

Don't forget to consider that these physical symptoms may be a warning that something is wrong health wise. Be sure to have a check-up if you have concerns, especially if your symptoms persist. It's important to take responsibility for your health.

Take a Break and Manage Stress

Research has highlighted how important it is to take a break at regular intervals throughout the day. When a 3 month survey was undertaken at Sheffield University by Professor Stafford, (results published 2013-2014) involving 850,000 people they found that responses, rapid perception and decision-making was better and more effective when people avoided cramming intensively and applied a looser, more relaxed approach.

Let's have a look at the relevance of breaks as a way to manage stress:

- We all have a twenty-four hour body clock that regulates how we function and supports us as we walk, exercise and undertake our daily tasks throughout the day. It also regulates our internal processes too, like healing, cell renewal, digestion, detoxifying. Taking a 15-20 minutes break approximately every 90 minutes allows our internal functions to occur effectively. If we regularly ignore the need for some down time we can become stressed, over tired, lose concentration, feel irritable, experience nausea and become vaguely unwell.

- A break can introduce a fresh perspective into a situation. When we're too close to something it can be difficult to see any other way of doing it. A break provides physical distance, fresh air, time out from the intense focus and level of concentration. It's often the time when new ideas or an alternative solution can appear.

- People are often encouraged to eat lunch away from their desk in order to freshen up and take a break from their work. Some people fear that they will waste valuable, productive time if they leave their desk or they may only want to take a short lunch break. But eating a healthy lunch, perhaps having a quick walk outside, some fruit, a drink of water, has been proven to improve productivity on return. A twenty-minute break can provide enough time to nourish and rehydrate, allow stress levels to subside and a calmer mental perspective to be introduced.

- Many over-worked, stressed people find that they are irritable with family and friends, have no time for anything other than work, don't sleep too well, are preoccupied. And yet the reason they started working so hard was probably to provide well for their family, enjoy a better quality of life, find job satisfaction and achieve some success. Balance can return by taking a break, learning to say no, delegating to others, forming alliances with other professionals in complementary fields who can share the load whilst giving each other support.

- Taking a break in the evening can mean going for a walk whilst the evening meal is cooking. Share time with family and friends and dedicate quality time to those relationships. Turn off the computer, put the phone onto silent for a couple of hours before bed and allow time to relax, wind down and mentally prepare for a good night's sleep. If work involves a lot of mental effort try to complement that by scheduling some physical exertion like going to the gym, having a run or a game of tennis or football. If work is hard physically then try to find time for mental activities like puzzles, games and reading. This supports a good, balanced state of mind and body.

A little planning and reorganisation can introduce a better work/life balance so that every part of life becomes less stressful, more enjoyable and positive. Taking a break can help you to manage stress and improve your quality of life.

Four Questions before You Plan Changes and Resolutions

How do you get on with your New Year's resolutions? If you did decide to make some this year the chances are that as the year progresses they will gradually fall beside the wayside. Why do you think that is, why do you think so many resolutions fail within the first month?

It's often the case that people make resolutions for half-baked or even unhelpful reasons. They may think they should use New Year as the opportunity to improve; after all, others are making resolutions. They may be wanting to lose weight, stop smoking, not drink as much so why not join in with others? Let's do it together and motivate each other.

Then let's not forget the suggestions that may have come from other people, the intention being that we'll improve through learning a new skill, make forward-looking plans, set exciting challenges to please/impress/satisfy family and friends!

Whilst these might be laudable enough reasons to consider, there are four good questions to ask yourself before you decide on which resolutions or changes to introduce into your life. These questions can help you to decide if you really want and are sufficiently motivated enough to introduce those changes.

- **Are you doing it for you?** The best motivation comes from doing something which enthuses and energizes you, makes you feel determined to improve. When other people try to force, demand, guilt-trip a change it can cause resentment and even rebelliousness as a reaction to their insistence. Motivation is sustained when you feel and want to do something because it's right for you.

- **Are you prepared to pace yourself?** You might be planning to stop smoking or drinking as much alcohol, want to lose weight, change a bad habit. Some people may succeed in achieving their goal all in one go, but you may need time to cut down, make adjustments to your life, get used to the new regimen. Pace yourself and do it in the way that's best for you.

- **Are you good at giving yourself credit?** Each success, each 'no' to a cigarette, drink or cream cake, each visit to the gym or time when you turn your phone off so that you can finish work a little earlier are all successes. Give yourself credit and savour the moment, the different mind-set you introduced at that time. Say 'well done' to yourself and enjoy how good you feel.

- **How you treat yourself if you fail?** Don't be too hard on yourself if you slip up at times. Treat yourself with the same kindness you would another person, and simply determine to start again. There's no need to wait for the next New Year or even the next new day. Decide to start again immediately and get back on track.

It can sometimes be tempting to tell ourselves 'it's not worth it', 'it's too hard', 'I can't do it'. But by using these four questions as guidelines we can gain insight into our true aspirations and introduce positive changes into our lives, changes for the better. Then we can start to do the things that have meaning for us, the things we want to do, that we're able to fully commit to, that suit us well.

Move Out of Your Comfort Zone and Grow

It can be tempting to stay in the safety of our familiar routines and activities. After all, there is already enough stress in the world. Why would we choose to add to our load, our stresses and responsibilities? However, it can be more stressful to be in a rut, aware that the days are passing, that we're not getting any younger and realise that nothing is going to change unless we actively do something about it.

Get out of your comfort zone for many reasons:

- It's important to intermittently experience the stress of testing ourselves by aiming to do well. Even if things do not work out as we might have hoped we can still learn from the experience, develop new skills and experience the buzz of adrenalin and the heightened state of awareness that comes from moving into new skills sets, areas and opportunities.

- When we start to extend our knowledge and become more experienced we make new contacts, friends and colleagues. This is valuable from both a personal and professional perspective. New people often bring new connections and information into our lives. You never know where they may lead!

- Improving our reputation by introducing ourselves to others and learning additional skills is an important way of keeping ourselves in the public eye. Refreshing our profile, being seen at a variety of events, talking and being friendly to others is all part of maintaining and enhancing our image. We demonstrate that we are interested, up-to-date and energetic, which are all good qualities to be associated with.

- If we stay within the safe confines of our comfort zone, with what we already know, we will never discover what we might have achieved with a little extra effort. Many top professionals, business people, athletes have all experienced failure and setbacks, but in order to get to the top they have stayed with the plan, endured disappointments and persevered. And often the toughest experiences are the most beneficial of all. Many people say that they learn more from their failures than from their successes.

- Even if we achieve a less than perfect result, moving out of our comfort zone can provide the launch pad for each stage of our journey to success. This platform can introduce the next opportunity for development, highlight what needs to be done next, precipitate a further plan of action. Moving into new situations can bring unexpected opportunities into our lives.

- Other people respect a trier. If they see someone having a go they will often try to help and will certainly respect a person for their efforts. And people are often generous with their information, contacts and help when they see someone who is genuinely trying hard to achieve something special.

The triumphant and elated feeling of achieving something out of our comfort zone is exciting. Accomplishing something special and unexpected, knowing and respecting how much we have achieved, and then, wondering where it may lead to next!

New Situations can be Stressful at First

We've all had many experiences of being new to a situation. The first day at junior school, moving up to 'big' school, starting a new job, our first date or our first kiss have all, no doubt, been times of apprehension and uncertainty. We want to make a good impression, be accepted and not make any silly mistakes. Those early experiences can shape our confidence and self-esteem for future occasions when we will be required to put ourselves into brand new situations and do well.

Some people thrive on stressful, first time situations. They love the adrenalin rush they get when they are under pressure. They don't stress about it going well or not. They are so charged with excitement and exhilaration that they're positive and pragmatic about whatever the eventual outcome may be.

But for others, new situations can be unexpectedly stressful:

- Being newly single after having been involved in a long-term relationship can be daunting. Not only is there the recovery process to go through, there is also the fact that being a single person means all future decisions and arrangements will have to be made alone from now on. Just the thought of having to find a home, furnish it, organise utilities, get equipment to work can be exhausting. Take the time to do it in stages, maybe rent at first and gradually discover where you want to live. Let friends or family help. They are often pleased to be asked. Trust that it will all come together in due course.

- Being new to the dating scene can be hard work, especially after a breakup or divorce. Going out socially and having to start all over again, smiling and making small talk can be too much for some people. Joining groups, a gym, classes, in a bid to circulate and make friends can be stressful at first. It can seem that everyone knows each other in these places, and in truth they probably do. Our own vulnerability can make us feel nervous or suspect that the people we meet are hostile and in their own friendship cliques. Making an effort to smile, be friendly and persevere will ensure that in time others get to know us, warm to and become friendly towards us.

- A new neighbourhood can feel strange initially. Not knowing where anything is, the bus routes, the post office can take time. Why not start by asking one or two of your new neighbours round for coffee? They will most likely be curious to meet you and keen to have a nosy and see how you've furnished your home. Many people are happy to show a new person the ropes, and it's always an advantage to have friendly people prepared to give advice, collect a parcel or help out whenever it's needed.

- The first day at a new job can be unnerving. Everyone else knows where the facilities are, where the good place is to buy lunch, how the different pieces of equipment work. Co-workers will all be friendly with each other and have lots of in-jokes and anecdotes, maybe with affectionate stories about your predecessor. Take time, keep your own counsel and be wary of revealing too much personal information in a bid to make friends. Work is an important place to protect oneself and ones' reputation, especially in the early days.

We all have to open ourselves up to new experiences at times. Even staying in the same place is no guarantee of things staying the same. Companies restructure, relationships end, people advance in their careers. Life is a process of change, but some scary experiences can be scary in a good way. We can't fight change, so learning to relish the opportunities it brings and understand more about ourselves can be a positive outcome from new situations.

Do Less and Enjoy it More

Often we feel compelled to rush from one activity to the next, leading such busy lives with many demands on our time and energy, trying to cram everything into each day. We may feel it's only right and proper to commit 100% effort to everything we do and whilst it's important to invest fully in our activities, sometimes doing a little less gives us the opportunity to enjoy things all the more.

Think about Christmas or Thanksgiving with all that turkey. We can end up eating turkey for days, in curry, salad, pie, sandwiches, and often would be happy if we never saw turkey again after such an excess of it. Or those who grow their own apples end up, at certain times of the year, eating apple with everything. It's far better to freeze some of the apples, or make pies, strudels and sauces that will be enjoyed throughout the year, rather than try to eat them all at once. Pacing ourselves and having less but over a longer period makes it more enjoyable and appreciated.

Let's look at areas where doing a little less can ensure that we enjoy it more.

- **Exercise**. We can keep on doing what we have always done, increasing the weights, attending more classes, setting ourselves even tougher challenges. Over time, though, this can become a problem, where the thought of exercise becomes unpleasant and something that we dread or don't enjoy. Instead of pushing to do a tough ten-mile walk why not sometimes give yourself a break and go for half the distance with an enjoyable pub lunch as a treat. Goals and challenges are important as a means of motivating and inspiring, but enjoying what we do is what keeps us on track over time.

- **Socializing**. Some people are out every night. They have busy social lives, dining out, partying and generally being seen around. It's often great fun, but gradually all those nights out can begin to blur and merge together, so becoming less enjoyable. Boredom and nonchalance can set in. Theatre and concert visits can be a pleasant way to spend an evening but some people attend that many shows that they can't remember which ones they've seen. They're unable to recall with affection the different events. Sometimes taking time to be more selective and dress up for an occasional evening out can be far more enjoyable. It becomes more of a special event and can be treasured as a result.

- **Networking** is often done with enthusiasm, especially by people new to business. They want to meet everyone, introduce themselves everywhere, make their mark. However, it is often more effective to pace meeting new people and take it at a slightly slower rate, taking time to cultivate proper relationships with the relevant people met at each event. Following up from meetings by having coffees and regular catch-ups is time consuming but is more effective that rushing from one network meeting to the next. Proper relationships are developed by taking the time to get to know, like and trust people. Nurturing good relationships is the key to success in business.

- **Treats** are great fun. But a treat is only a treat when it is an occasional, special indulgence. Chocolate is the classic treat, but equally a bunch of flowers, saving up to buy something that is really yearned for, giving a gift that has particular significance are all the stuff of treats. Good quality chocolate, savoured and enjoyed is a lovely pleasure at times. Eat too much and it is bad for us. Having things as treats means that when we do indulge we enjoy them all the more.

And that is the key to satisfaction and enjoyment. Pacing ourselves, giving ourselves challenges at times, but being aware of doing things at a comfortable pace enables us to commit to what we do, enjoy it and get the most out of each experience. It is a most positive way to live, doing less but enjoying it more.

When Things Don't Go to Plan

How many of us feel under pressure to be perfect? I certainly see lots of clients who dread the prospect of their arrangements going wrong, who regard things not going to plan as letting themselves or others down, who check minute details repeatedly to ensure that everything is correct.

Life can be frustrating. We may take great care, prepare for every eventuality and still life doesn't always go to plan. How many people prepare meticulously for their wedding day, a special event, an exam, the birth of their baby only for something to happen that completely throws all their arrangements into disarray?

When things don't go to plan we have to be pragmatic, retain a sense of humour, quickly devise an alternative. And importantly, learning from life's upheavals and curved balls can provide the most memorable, significant times in our lives.

Let's consider what can happen when things don't work out as we would have hoped:

- **Work;** many of us learn a lot about ourselves and our capabilities, gain valuable insights into our colleagues when things don't go to plan. We discover how tenacious we can be, how valuable our contacts are, how helpful and supportive our work colleagues are. The most beneficial lessons in work occur when things go wrong and we have to access our inner resources to find a solution. Our most difficult clients are our best teachers; they take us out of our comfort zone and improve our competency and experience.

- **Social;** the best, most memorable times are often the occasions when things went wrong. No one ever remembers the perfect day when everything went smoothly. It's the picnic in the rain, the soggy sandwiches, the cows chasing them across a meadow, the waiter spilling the drinks that people laugh and reminisce about with affection years later.

- **Health;** we may be conscientious about our diet, take care to exercise regularly but there are times when things don't go too well and we fall ill. What's that about? Might it be that unconsciously we've decided that whatever we had planned isn't right for us and our unconscious is making the decision on our behalf? Might it be that we need a break or that we are doing something for the wrong reasons and need to become more assertive or walk away? Pay attention to your inner responses and learn to listen to what's going on at these times.

- **Relationships;** these are an important part of our life. Lovers, friends and family all add so much to our lives; companionship, support, sometimes a steadying hand or a calming voice can keep us grounded and on track. When things don't go to plan in our relationships it may be time to weigh up all the different factors. Are we being treated fairly, do we need to communicate more effectively, are we appropriately assertive? These questions address our self-esteem, confidence and self-worth and it may be that we need to acknowledge and deal with old, repeating patterns in our relationships that are not serving us well.

Not everything in life needs to go to plan all the time. Indeed things going off plan can sometimes be a blessing in disguise and lead us in an unexpected direction, introducing us to a wonderful new phase in our lives. Sometimes though it can be a time when we need to assess what's going on in our lives and maybe take stock of our levels of control. When things don't go to plan it may indicate that it's time to start work on improving ourselves and our responses to people and situations.

Sometimes it's Important to Say 'I Have Had Enough'

Patterns in relationships start from the minute we meet someone. Two people often establish their own dynamic in the earliest days of their relationship. This is why the phrase 'start as you mean to go on' is so important. It becomes more difficult to change any patterns we don't like when they have been in place for a while.

Let's look at the different areas of our lives:

- **Work.** When we start a new job we are keen to impress, to justify the faith shown in hiring us. We want to prove that we are enthusiastic, competent and capable and are prepared to turn our hand to many things. Often, though, we can end up working longer and longer hours.

  It may be that we are being taken advantage of. Or perhaps other people do not appreciate our workload and how much we have to do. A further reason may be that we are especially conscientious and are afraid of making a mistake or are not quite sure what to do and are taking our time to work it out. It is important to communicate our situation to our manager in order to introduce a better balance. Otherwise stress can accumulate and cause our work to suffer.

- **Home**. Our home is meant to be a peaceful haven, a place where we return to relax. Often, though, life comes with problems. Sometimes men may find that they have work, financial or business problems that they do not want to burden their family with. Women often try to multi-task and be superwoman, aiming to run the home and do everything in a smooth, almost invisible way so that others are unaware of the amount of effort involved.

  Sometimes saying, 'I have had enough, I need some help' can be an important way of allowing others to understand what is going on and invite their help. They can't offer if they don't know what's needed.

- **Relationships**. When we're married, settled in a relationship with a special someone, we want to please them and make them happy. Sometimes the effort can seem one-sided, with one person feeling that it's always them who makes the compromises. Or, over time one person may realise that they're never going to work out their differences and it's time to admit that they've had enough.

  Relationship counselling may be able to help in understanding each other better and communicating more effectively. But sometimes breaking up becomes the best option as it enables both people to try for happiness in their lives and start again.

- **Friends** are supposed to be the people with whom we relax, share our fun and free time with. But sometimes friends take advantage. One person may find that they're the regular driver, organiser, caterer, person who pays. Speaking out and insisting that other people take their turn is important. And doing this allows others to commit and invest in the friendship equally.

There are times when it's important to speak up and say how we feel. If we begin to sense that there's an imbalance it can be important to address this before resentment and anger start to fester, causing bad feelings and damage to the relationship. We have to take responsibility for how we allow people to treat us and that can be a big part of any problems.

Sometimes there can be a fear of being seen to be not coping or of being less than perfect and that can inhibit us from saying that we've had enough. Finding the courage to say how we feel, explain what's going on and ask for help can be surprisingly well-received. People usually understand and are often happy to help if they are given the chance.

Six Tips for Dealing with Rough Patches

We all experience times in life when things don't go to plan. There may be one area which causes serious hurt and disappointment or perhaps even a sequence of setbacks in several areas of our life where we lose our support network, become overwhelmed or feel under-resourced about what to do to improve the situation.

There are a few things we can do to help at these times:

- Acknowledge that rarely does everything 'urgent' have to be dealt with at once. It's useful to take a step back and identify the key, most pressing items that need immediate attention. Then perhaps something as simple as a phone call may be enough to ease the load, may placate the other party for the time being by reassuring them that you're aware of the situation and are dealing with it promptly.

- Can someone else be brought in to help with certain aspects of the issue? Other people are often happy to be included and may even contribute a new and different perspective. Their involvement may help you feel supported, less alone and better able to manage the stress.

- Take care of yourself. A rough patch can threaten your self-esteem, cause you to feel inadequate, that you can't cope, are perhaps a failure in some way. Take care to protect your self-esteem and associate with supportive people, family, friends, colleagues who believe in you, who are prepared to reassure you that you are skilled, talented, capable, likeable and that this rough patch will pass. Make time for hobbies, interests and activities that you do well, that reinforce the belief that you're talented and successful in many areas of your life.

- Rough patches can teach us a great deal. It feels good when things go well, but those times often occur within our comfort zone. The difficult experiences in life, the failures and disappointments are often the times that we reflect on in later years as having been our important learning opportunities. In order to come through rough patches we may need to learn new skills, tailor our expectations and prepare more thoroughly so that we improve our future chances of success.

- There may be a requirement to learn better ways of doing things. We may need external help by way of training in order to learn new skills and better strategies, a business coach may help us to focus on a more effective plan, a counsellor or hypnotherapist may provide valuable personal healing and development opportunities. Value the space that a setback or rough patch provides to develop a more positive, structured, focused way of moving forward in your life.

- Avoid replaying a negative mind-set over and over again. When we're used to success or have invested a lot of ourselves in a particular outcome it can be a bitter blow to our self-esteem if things don't go to plan. If that situation in compounded by further setbacks it can be difficult to see beyond those disappointments. Resist the temptation to beat yourself up and replay the negative story repeatedly. It can become a destructive habit, eroding hope, energy and enthusiasm for future opportunities.

Introduce distractions, mini-breaks, times when you perhaps arrange to have fun, interesting conversation, or even book some therapy to allow yourself to heal any negativity and disappointment. Then prepare to go and start anew. Recover your self-belief and enjoy utilising all the lessons learned for this, the new stage of your journey to success.

Do Things You Don't Want to do Sometimes

We live in an age where there is much emphasis placed on doing only what we want to do, on the importance of being assertive about what is right for us. We're taught that we should only make choices that feel good, that we should live the dream. And indeed, these points are crucial in being true to ourselves.

But equally, personal responsibility also means having balance in life, being aware of the requirement to co-exist harmoniously with others. It's important not to lose sight of the bigger picture, the fact that there are often other people who need consideration, who live alongside us and who also have their own needs, wishes and rights. Sharing, doing things together, co-operating and working out a schedule may well require negotiation, compromise and a little selflessness.

- Doing things we don't want to do sometimes takes us out of our comfort zone and ensures that we try new activities, visit places, meet people we perhaps might not have otherwise met. Whatever happens, whether it be ultimately a good or a bad experience we can find it interesting that we have had a go at something new and different.

- It lets other people know that their wishes are being listened to and considered as valid and worthwhile. Being inflexible and adamant that we only ever do what we want to do may sound fine in principle but realistically it can be good to share each other's lives and interests. Even if we only occasionally agree to do something we don't want to do and join them in their activities, it's good to convey to our partner that we're sufficiently interested in spending time together doing what they want sometimes. It demonstrates empathy, support and a willingness to work at the relationship.

- It can be a good lesson in life to introduce restraint and do something other than what we want to do at times. Personal discipline is an important life skill and we need to be able to cope appropriately with refusal, rejection and not getting our own way all the time. We need to be able to react in an adult manner, with grace and humility when we effectively meet a brick wall, a dead-end and things do not go our way.

- An act of kindness and selflessness can demonstrate respect and support for a friend, colleague or neighbour. By making time to do something you may not wish to do but which others would like, you make a valuable gesture, especially when it's of importance to them. Giving a little time, physical or emotional support and attention when they need it can mean far more than an expensive gift. Thoughtfulness and consideration are priceless.

It's important to remember that not everything in life is about us; other people have a right to consideration, fair play and having their turn. Doing things we don't want to do sometimes can be a way to demonstrate an important level of humility, insight and sensitivity.

Then there's the stress of financial setbacks, something that many households have to endure. Let's look at some ways to help manage that stress, and consider the role that money and wealth can have in our lives.

Things to Consider Before Your Debt Spirals Out of Control

For many homes the dread of being seriously in debt is never very far away, in many cases only the latest pay cheque being between them and homelessness. A change in interest rates, divorce, the loss of overtime or bonus payments can literally throw a tightly managed household into tragedy.

Let's consider some things that may be able to help before your debt spirals out of control:

- Concern at what friends, family, colleagues might say or think is often an initial knee-jerk reaction to a reduction in disposable income and spending power. Fear of looking a failure, being diminished in other people's eyes can cause otherwise sensible, rational people to hide the truth from others, sometimes even from their partners.

- Many people have money issues but find that when they share their problems with partners who understand and want to help they're able to deal with a difficult financial situation sooner rather than later, before debt starts to mount up excessively. Keeping up appearances can result in rash over-spending and further exacerbation of the problem.

- Detail and check the household expenses. Many people automatically pay standing orders without thinking too much about them. Appliance insurances, unused memberships may be able to be rationalised and let go. Investigate changing onto cheaper tariffs, using more efficient providers, shopping at less expensive stores.

- There may be unconsidered ways of earning money. Many homes have wardrobes full of quality, hardly worn clothes that have simply been outgrown or become outdated or stacks of unused gadgets and appliances stored away in the garage or spare room. These items could be sold online or at a car boot sale.

What about a skill or talent such as cake making, gardening, decorating that others would be happy to pay for, that could be done part-time, as and when is convenient. Time is something that many people are short of. Offering to help with their time constraints might support a new source of income; things like shopping, collecting children, running errands could support a time-strapped family and earn a little extra money.

- Credit cards can be used excessively when income is tight. They're often viewed as money in reserve, as spare available cash until the statements start to arrive and the balance in unable to be reduced. When only minimum payments are made it's virtually impossible to pay off more than the monthly interest; it's like treading water, just about keeping afloat. Speaking to card providers and other creditors like mortgage providers and utilities that are proving hard/impossible to pay sooner rather than later is important.

The sole aim of creditors is to get their money back in the most efficient way. Speaking to them as early as possible enables a realistic plan of repayment to be implemented. It's in no one's interests to institute court proceedings so pick up the phone, explain the situation and make an offer to pay what you can afford. Mortgage providers are often prepared to go onto 'interest only' arrangements where they receive the borrowed capital when the property is eventually sold.

- Share with friends that you're cutting back a little on your spending. Real friends will be happy to see you for a pasta supper and a bottle of wine at home and not miss the expensive restaurant or they would enjoy a cup of coffee instead of a cafe lunch. It may be a relief for them to scale down their dining out budget too.

Girls nights in can be dedicated to fun pampering sessions instead of booking spa treatments at beauty salons.

- Children are often a major part of household expenses and children's education is often the reason why families choose to live where they do; the catchment area for good schools can be seriously reflected in local house prices. Sometimes though there may need to a discussion about the impact such a heavy financial commitment is having on the household budget. School fees, uniform, trips, expenses all add together to erode disposable income and may leave the family unable to survive financially. Investigate the possibility of other good schools nearby; do you know anyone who goes there, how easy might it be to change, how might you approach that discussion with your children?

Debt can catch us unawares. Something that was just about manageable can gradually spiral and become out-of-control. There are several advisory bodies in the UK that are willing to help. The Citizens Advice Bureau and the National Debt Line are two bodies available to discuss individual cases, but all advice starts with protecting your home, reducing overheads, being honest and facing the fact that this problem needs to be dealt with as soon as possible, before it gets any bigger.

Inexpensive Ways to Enhance Your Life and Have Fun

There is frequent talk in the media about people who struggle with increasing debt that will take years for them to repay, often taking their relationships and families to the brink of disaster. Let's look at some ways to help this situation, at inexpensive ways to enhance your life whilst still having a good time.

- **Accept invitations,** You may feel embarrassed at going to other people's events if you're not in a position to reciprocate or take an expensive gift, but people invite you because they want to spend time with you. Be good company, relax and contribute with your presence. A good guest is an important part of any successful event.

- **Invite people to yours**. Ask people to bring a contribution with them. Most people don't mind bringing a dish or a bottle and it means that you all have a good time with relatively little effort or expense. Or if you're friendly with your neighbours have a safari supper with one course at each person's house, walking from one venue to the next.

- **Party games** are an inexpensive way of entertaining guests. Charades, board games, cards are a fun way to spend an afternoon or evening with friends and many people love getting to know each other better as they chat, share banter and play to win. Often these evenings become a regular, eagerly anticipated part of the social calendar.

- **Spend time with children**. Watching, playing with the children of family and friends is great fun. Their ability to enjoy themselves, play the same game over and over again, often requiring little or no financial outlay is delightful. Children's spontaneous laughter is one of the most delightful sounds in the world.

- **People-watch over a cup of coffee** in a shopping mall. It's a fascinating way to spend an hour or two, inventing stories about people's lives, watching the world go by.

- **Go for a walk.** Parks, the beach, woodland are often free to enjoy and for the price of petrol or a bus ride can be relatively accessible. Enjoy a brisk walk on your own or ask friends with children or a dog to join you. Maybe come home to a mug of hot chocolate, a slow-cooker casserole or a lovely relaxing bath.

- **Make your home a cosy haven**. Candles, colourful prints, bright cushions in an assortment of fabrics can make your home or bedroom a lovely retreat to relax and enjoy whilst not costing a great deal of money. Keep your place clean and tidy; that in itself can help you to feel more positive about your home and yourself. Play music, read a book and enjoy having time for yourself.

- **Smile**. Remember the things in your life that you can be grateful for. Whether it be your home, your health, the difficulties you have overcome, the people you have met along the way, many of us can pause, reflect and be grateful for much in our lives.

Starting out again, being newly single can be incredibly hard and generate an inordinate amount of stress. Income and spending power may have become a serious consideration, friends may have scattered for a variety of reasons. Being newly single can also highlight self-esteem and confidence related issues. Here are some pointers for being alone but not lonely.

Newly Single and Those Significant Times of the Year

When we are unexpectedly left alone, either through death or divorce it can precipitate a long, painful process of healing and recovery. One person cannot fully appreciate what another is going through, no matter how understanding they may try to be. Time and reconciliation about what has happened are the keys to survival and moving on. Often, though, significant dates and anniversaries will continue to remind us of what we have lost, of what we are missing in our lives.

There are particular times in the year when being alone is especially hard. Christmas, Bank Holidays, long weekends, Valentine's Day as well as more personal anniversaries can be poignant times which serve to underline our newly single status. Family and friends may be supportive, but cannot fully appreciate the diverse emotions experienced at these times.

Here are some tips to help with your newly single status:

- At those times of the year when the whole world seems to be in love, involved in happy relationships and spending quality time together it's important to grieve for what you no longer have in your life. Be gentle with yourself and accept that it can take time to heal and become strong enough to be able to look back and smile at the happy memories, the fun times you shared together. Acknowledge the sad times, the times when you are especially aware of your aloneness and if the tears come, allow them space to express how you're feeling.

- **Determine to treat yourself with love** and pamper yourself over those long weekends too. Buy your favourite food, organise lovely things for yourself, arrange indulgent treatments, source a book you've always wanted to read, a favourite film. Turn time that could be painful, lonely or negative into a pleasant, gentle occasion. Then settle down and enjoy some quality 'me' time. Being kind to yourself when you feel vulnerable is important.

- **Allow other people to help**. Friends and family may be able to offer important support at difficult times of the year. Let them know if you're feeling especially fragile and allow them to help. If they invite you to join them, be appreciative and allow them to include you in their plans. Sometimes invitations can lead to interesting new directions or opportunities to form new friendships.

- **Identify groups that interest you** and join them. Not everyone is in or indeed wants to be in a relationship. Many groups have activities that are deliberately scheduled for Bank Holidays and Valentine's Day. By joining an interesting group you meet like-minded people, potential new friends and maybe a new partner eventually, whilst, at the same time, keeping busy doing the things that appeal to you.

- **Work on improving your personal confidence levels.** Maybe undertake counselling or hypnotherapy to support your healing, deal with the emotions and enable yourself to become stronger and more positive as a result. Your commitment to therapy can help you to learn from your experience, reconcile what you have been through and emerge as a stronger more rounded person.

- Some people find it beneficial to have a special memorial, especially at significant times of the year, like birthdays, anniversaries and Christmas. Valentine's Day can also be a poignant time, particularly if a soul mate has left your life. Holding a service or ritual can provide comfort and can sometimes be more effective if it's done in private. It can be a personal way to remember the other person and acknowledge the important role they had in your life.

Finding a loving relationship, a special someone brings colour and joy into our lives. Sharing our time, life, hopes and dreams with that special person, only to then lose them may require a long period of healing and readjustment. Over time we aim to become strong and able to start again with our life, a little older, wiser and more experienced than before.

CHAPTER TWO

Stress and Work

Ways to Help With Your Work/Life Balance

There are times when our commitment to a positive work/life balance can be affected and we start to feel stressed, resentful and frustrated with life. Our time may be required to deal with an urgent work situation, staffing levels may be inadequate or we find that it's important for us to intervene in a domestic matter and we become stressed through being pulled in many different directions. If this is an occasional or emergency situation we may be able to accommodate it for a while.

However, if this becomes a way of life, goes on for too long or becomes our regular fire-fighting response we may need to look at other options to support a better work/life balance and bring some peace of mind and harmony back into our lives. Hypnotherapy can help reintroduce a better sense of balance and support the ability to cope in a happier, more positive, less reactive way.

- **Balance** in life starts by taking care of you, by looking after yourself nutritionally, stopping for regular, healthy food breaks, water, exercise, fresh air and fun. When we're stressed and out of balance it can affect our quality of sleep, libido, sense of humour, positive perspective, ability to cope. Start by weighing up what's really important to you, what you need to support your ability to take good care of you and enable you to maintain a healthy balance in the different areas of your life.

Recognise that there may be a need for additional help. Consider paying for cleaning, laundry or gardening to be done by someone else. Delegate tasks or ask for help and even if they're not done to your exacting standards, relax and appreciate the input.

- **Learn to say 'no' sometimes**. It can be tempting to appear ready and willing to do everything that's asked of you, happy to take on more and more work or accept invitations to every function you're invited to but sometimes it's important to weigh up the pros and cons of these different requests. Small businesses understandably often have a feast or famine mind-set. When work requests come in they're often automatically accepted because of the requirement to earn money and establish good relationships with existing or potentially new customers and clients.

But learning to say 'no' sometimes can help you to maximise on the use of your time and energy. It enables you to use them in the best possible way, to look after your existing business well, focus on what's right for you, prioritise, give each piece of work, offer or opportunity your full consideration and focus clearly on how it meets your long-term goals.

'No' can teach co-workers, family and friends not to rely on you for everything and, if necessary, to become a little more independent in their thinking and more confident in their own abilities. It also teaches them that whilst at times you may be amenable to their suggestions, go along with their wishes and/or demands, you are also deserving of respect, entitled to have opinions of your own and have a say in any decisions, plans and arrangements.

- **Do what feels right for you**. Are your motives on track or are you over-committing in order to be seen as popular, busy or indispensable? Take some quiet time and check what your gut, your inner voice is saying. Taking on too much or agreeing to do things we don't really want to do may take us out of our comfort zone and encourage us to develop and grow, but the motivation to maintain that effort comes from the excitement, enthusiasm and positivity we feel in following genuine, heartfelt goals, hopes and dreams.

- **Put yourself in your diary** on a regular basis, just like you would an important client. Plan some quiet time, time to read a book or to go for a pleasant walk in the countryside or to the beach. Arrange a spa day where you have to leave your phone behind and are unavailable to be contacted unless there's a real emergency. Make time to enjoy your hobbies and interests.

- **Decide to finish work at a reasonable time**. Turn off your work phone and computer. Be strict about it, dedicating time to yourself, your family and your friends. These personal areas deserve to be treated as important, respected and valued by you in order for them to thrive and enjoy significance in your life, so that you achieve a healthy work/life balance.

Too Busy to Take a Holiday From Work?

Did you know that 19 million days of annual leave remain untaken in the UK every year? And that figure doesn't include the sole traders, small businesses and the self-employed who regularly forgo holidays for fear of missing out on sales and business opportunities. Or they are worried about being unavailable and disappointing their clients.

Do you miss out on your annual leave, feel nervous at leaving the office, work increasingly longer hours, perhaps even calling in at work over the weekend? You may not regard yourself as a workaholic yet find yourself regularly working late to finish essential paperwork or feel that you're not ready to leave work 'just yet'?

Some people define themselves through their job; it's how they think of themselves. Life can become more complicated once family, friends and relationships become involved. There isn't a job description or a set of rules provided for home life. Sometimes it can seem less messy, be the easier option to become immersed in work; after all, there's always something to be busy with.

Also leaving the office for an extended period can require someone else to take charge, become acquainted with what's going on. This can feel a vulnerable position to be in, as letting go of the reins may mean someone discovering errors and omissions, coming up with new, innovative ideas or doing a better job.

But working unremittingly and being too busy to take a holiday can bring problems and issues that eventually require attention, not least of which can be stress and burnout.

Let's look at some ways to introduce a better perspective and deal with being too busy to take time off work:

- **Check if family and friends are becoming upset** and exasperated because you spend weekends regularly checking your phone and emails 'just in case'? Or when on holiday do you spend the first three days stressed and worrying about what's happening whilst you're away and the last three days revving up again? Remember, these are the important people in your life, the ones who really care about you. Share your work-related concerns with them, let them be supportive, plan to start spending quality time together and learn to relax and have fun.

- **Some people thrive on the adrenalin rush** they get from being busy. The sense of urgency from taking on vast quantities of work, having pressurised deadlines or demanding clients who expect immediate results can be exciting and elevate thinking and responses to heightened levels of awareness. Also small businesses are often apprehensive at turning down work for fear of losing clients. But living in a constant state of stress can result in an inability to switch off, cause the mind to continually race. This can start to impact on health and well-being, causing burnout to occur.

- **Inject some realism** into your way of working. Accept that you can only do so much, that you can't be all things to all men, agree to every demand from your customers or accept every order for work. Saying 'yes' can sometimes mean that you commit too much time and energy to something that is not viable. Get to know other businesses with whom you can liaise and effectively out-source work they'd be better suited to. Who knows, you may all end up building better, more valuable customer bases through mutual cooperation with those in similar, complementary fields.

- **Work on your confidence**, your self-belief and remind yourself that you're doing the best you can. Keep on top of your CPD so that you feel confident in your skills. It's important to earn a living and be professional but accept that you're human and need to take a holiday sometimes. Ensure there's work that you enjoy, that gives you satisfaction when you go to the office each day.

- **Build good relationships** with clients and customers so that you can help each other in times of crisis. Then if you're overloaded, experience problems, delays or an occasional error you can discuss it and find the best solution. Communicate with mutual respect and understanding so that you can negotiate and establish honest and meaningful relationships.

- **Be aware of your personal signs of being stressed**. There are 360 physical symptoms of stress so learn to recognise your own warning signs. You may lose your sense of humour, become irritable or stop sleeping well. Some people over-eat for comfort or lose their appetite. Notice if your memory or concentration starts slipping or you start to experience headaches. These symptoms can alert you to the importance of taking a break, a holiday in order to refresh and recover from the pressures you're experiencing.

Being too busy to take a holiday may seem like proof of your success, a sign that you're doing well and are important, but taking a break gives you time to relax and recharge, spend time with the special people in your life and then return to work feeling energised to do a better job.

Is Work Too Important in Your Life?

Did you know that one in five people work an additional 7 hours a week in unpaid overtime on top of their paid hours? Is that dedication or folly! If you find that you come into this category, reflect for a moment on what else you could do with an extra day each week. Do you ever wonder if work is too important in your life?

Clearly work is an important part of all our lives, it provides us with purpose, challenge, occupation as well as necessary income, but, as the saying goes, 'no one ever said on their deathbed that they wished they'd spent more time at work'.

For many people work is about providing a roof over their heads, the means to take care of their children and family and to support their hobbies and interests. Whilst it's important for us to do something meaningful and satisfying with our time, it's also important that we nurture and safeguard the essential relationships and personal aspects of our lives too.

So, with that in mind, let's question how important work is to you:

- **Is your genius at work your curse at home?** Are your areas of particular competency, like rapid decision making, attention to detail and perfectionism regarded as overbearing and unwelcome at home? Find ways to 'park' those skills and relax your approach once you leave the office for the day.

- **Do you regularly agree to take on more work than you can handle?** I knew a top female executive whose job was in a male dominated environment. She refused to say 'no' to her boss when asked to take on additional tasks as she was concerned that she'd be regarded as weak or unequal to the job. She frequently worked late into the evening and at weekends.

  After addressing her confidence and self-worth she became more positive about her abilities and skills. One day her boss approached her about some urgent work he needed doing. She replied that she'd be happy to do it, but that she had several other projects in the pipeline; what order would he like them doing in, how would he suggest she proceed? It turned out that he was unaware of the extent of her demanding workload, was simply checking to see if she had any spare capacity and was happy to pass the task on to someone else.

  Learning to communicate better, remain calm and be appropriately assertive is the key to dealing with an excess of requests.

- **Do you fear that you're not up to the job,** are going to be 'found out' and because of this spend a lot of time double-checking your work? Do you take on an increasing number of tasks in a desperate bid to prove your worth to your boss? Doing a good job is important but being motivated by fear and anxiety is counter-productive and results in stress and anxiety which often causes more mistakes.

In these situations it's important to consider if extra training or education is needed to improve your confidence in your abilities. Reflect if this is the best job for you or are you under too much pressure? Question how frequently mistakes are made and whether or not they're serious. We all make occasional mistakes. Being kinder to ourselves allows us to be less than perfect, and reduces the fear and stress factor.

- **Are you afraid to delegate?** Some people work longer and longer hours because they're afraid of letting go of control, are concerned that others may do a better job or that they'll lose status or seniority.

  The reality though is that teaching others to do some of our work encourages enthusiasm and work satisfaction in our staff, provides opportunities for them to suggest ideas, innovations and improvements and frees us to do other, more important work, perhaps developing different areas of the business. It may even allow us to have a little free time!

- **Remind yourself about the reasons why you work so hard;** your family, friends, the important interests and relationships that you enjoy. These are probably a significant part of your motivation to work as hard as you do. Just because work shouts loudest, is important and demanding doesn't mean that you should ignore or relegate the other areas of your life into second place. Free time spent with the important people in your life, doing the things you enjoy enables you to recharge your batteries, reduce your stress levels and feel happier about yourself and your choices.

Nurturing your important friendships, relationships and interests whilst maintaining a good work/life balance means that you're better able to resume your work-related duties feeling refreshed and recharged, with better concentration and renewed vigour. Finishing work at a reasonable time, taking breaks and allowing yourself time to wind down after work all help you to successfully manage stress and burnout.

Time, One Thing You Can't Afford to Waste

So many people say they have no time, that there are not enough hours in the day and yet often, when they're really busy, are amazed, incredulous at how much they actually manage to achieve. The saying, 'if you want something doing ask a busy person' rings especially true. A busy person doesn't waste time procrastinating, mulling over where to start. They simply begin and do it.

With that in mind, let's look at ways to utilize your time more effectively:

- **Prioritize.** It can become a habit to instantly react to other people's emergencies and demands and, on occasion, that might be appropriate. It's reasonable to treat an important client with respect, to let them know that they're a top priority. After all, your quality customer service may have been a significant part of their reason for choosing to come to you in the first place. But even important clients have to appreciate that they're not the only call on your time. They have to treat you with respect and be reasonable in their requests.

  Prioritizing helps you to list the immediate, most pressing demands on your time. Order them in the most efficient way. Some tasks may be complex and require a lot of time, others may need to be undertaken in stages with input intermittently required from other service providers. These are important considerations to factor in. Make a comprehensive list in order to assess and prioritize the best way to proceed. Then, when any new demands are made upon you, you can modify your list and make sensible, realistic decisions. Using a list helps you organise your thoughts and prioritize your time more effectively.

- **Be constructive**. People typically fill their time with what needs to be done, so a simple task may take thirty minutes or be extended to fill half a day, depending on how much time there is available. Focus on the task in hand and commit to maximising your input. Then reward yourself with a short break.

  Notice how much time you fritter and waste. A five minute coffee break can take more than double that if you calculate the time spent walking to the kitchen, chatting, waiting for the kettle to boil. Watching the news can absorb another thirty minutes if you become distracted by reports on topical items. Calling at the local shop several times a day can further add to the amount of time wasted.

  It is important to have breaks. They help manage stress, provide a helpful interlude to reflect on problems and issues, give an opportunity to consider a different perspective and become calmer. Make the most of your breaks by including healthy food, water, fresh air, exercise. Use your time constructively.

- **Commit your full attention** to each task in turn and avoid being distracted. Some people switch their phone to silent, only check their emails and post at specific times so that they're able to concentrate fully. Then you're less likely to make mistakes, repeat work you've already done or lose track of where you're up to.

- **Delegate**. Some tasks may be able to be done satisfactorily by another person. Taking on a junior may initially mean having to spend time training or clarifying processes and procedures but that may be good practice in the long-term. Someone with a fresh pair of eyes may make valuable suggestions.

- **Sharing work or forming alliances** with other associated businesses may ease your workload by passing on tasks that are better suited to their skills. If they share some of their leads and contacts you could find that you're both able to offer an improved service to your combined clients.

- **Be efficient**. If you part-finish a piece of work make clear notes as to where you're up to, any actions that have been taken. It saves time when you eventually return to it. A clear, visible summary saves time, effort and potential embarrassment at looking inefficient.

  Implement systems that help you manage work efficiently. De-clutter regularly and archive old, outdated data away from more relevant operational paperwork.

- **Allow time for fun, relaxation, family and friends**. Make time for your special people and nurture those relationships. Let them be a significant part of your life and support network. They are often an important part of the reason why you work so hard.

Equally, allocate valuable time for yourself, just as you would a respected, valued client. Be sure to stop and give yourself credit when you've completed an important task or project. Enjoy each achievement rather than simply moving from one task to the next. It's important to value how you spend your time.

How Important is Your Image to You?

How many of us feel the pressure to present the right image? Even young people are acutely image conscious and brand aware. Try to persuade a young person to wear a cheaper make of supermarket own brand trainers; it would be regarded as the ultimate humiliation!

TV, magazines and social media treat sporting a particular make of clothes and accessories or using the latest technology as an essential part of having street cred. For young people this is especially important as it puts them on a par with others in their peer group, makes them feel they belong and maybe even elevates them to 'elitist level' if they're able to sustain each latest up-to-the-minute look.

Adults like to think they're less judgmental than young people. They're able to stand back and recognise that much of the pressure to look, act and conform to a particular style is media driven. Much of it is driven by the desire to make sales, to introduce new trends and products so that people buy more 'stuff' in order to be seen to be dynamic and up-to-date.

 Many adults would hate to be perceived as superficial or unduly affected by another's possessions, clothes or presentation of themselves, but image is often a significant factor in our relationships with others. We all make instant decisions, form instant impressions of people when we first meet.

And caring about our appearance, dressing well, looking after ourselves can be perceived as taking responsibility for ourselves as well as displaying good manners and consideration for the company we keep, whether it be for our partners, friends and family, employers, customers and clients. It demonstrates that we regard ourselves as important, we care enough to want to make a good impression and we're prepared to invest time, money and effort into looking good when we're committing to be with other people.

Wearing a smart suit, a pair of killer heels, a dash of lipstick, an expensive aftershave, having a beauty treatment or a new hairdo makes us feel much more confident, knowing that we're looking good. When we feel we look the part we're often able to raise our game and portray that positive persona. We stand taller and feel more in control.

However, putting ourselves under massive pressure to earn the money to sustain the expensive wardrobe, designer handbags, expensive homes, cars, holidays and school fees can put an inordinate amount of strain on our quality of life, relationships, health and wellbeing. Stopping and reflecting on what's important in life can sometimes result in spending less money and enjoying a camping trip rather than a 5 star luxury holiday, can prompt the decision to work fewer hours and come home earlier to be with our children in order to discuss what's happening in their lives.

Image pressure can cause a significant amount of personal stress. The pressure to be a certain body shape or size, exceptionally slim or muscular and ripped can cause body anxiety in young and old, male and female as they strive to eat less or work out more. The incidence of eating disorders, once seen as the province of young females, is escalating in young men and older people as they feel the pressure to look good through media-defined eyes.

Maintaining a positive look as we start to age is important too as part of our ongoing image and desire to be accepted in certain spheres of life. Feeling the pressure to look young, hide the signs of ageing can at times compel some of us to consider the need for surgical and non-surgical procedures, sometimes at great cost financially, physically and psychologically. Many people dye their hair to disguise evidence of their advancing years or spend time agonising over ways to hide the signs of their hair loss.

And, yes, fitting in, being received in a positive way, regarded as someone who is successful, attractive and professional can give an important boost to our confidence as we go about our daily lives. Wearing the right clothes, looking fit and attractive is often a key aspect of the impression we give. But is that really the way to measure the quality of our lives?

Some people feel extra confident when wearing a smart company uniform; it portrays a specific image, a corporate brand identity with all its associated professionalism. A uniform can bring a certain dignity and gravitas to a situation where staff find they feel positive through being part of the corporate team. Compulsory school uniform negates the need for schoolchildren to compete with each other over their daily clothing but the school uniform from a highly regarded school can be something that parents aspire to for the sake of their children; it conveys an elitist image.

But, that aside, let's not ignore the role that managing stress, looking after ourselves can play in our lives and work to sustain a healthy, positive way of life. A nutritious diet, regular exercise routine and stress-free lifestyle are all recognised as effective ways of taking good care of ourselves and counteracting the effects of ageing and excess. When asked what they found most attractive about others many people commented that it was their natural, relaxed manner, their infectious sense of humour and their kind nature that was most appealing!

Maybe we should devote more time and energy to learning ways to relax, to focus on what's really important in our lives and pay less heed to the pressures of advertising and the media when we decide what to wear, how to look and how to live our lives.

What First Impression Do You Give to Customers and Clients?

When we're in business for ourselves, and especially when we're long-established, it can be all too easy to lose sight of the impression our business conveys to existing and potential new clients and customers. We may be so preoccupied with completing the tasks in hand, making new contacts, winning actual orders that we forget to stop and pretend to be our own customer, evaluate how we look, review how our premises appear, consider the impression we convey.

Impressions, especially first impressions, can make all the difference to how our customers and clients interact with us. This is why some organisations hire secret shoppers, to gain feedback on their customers' experience of dealing with them. Their findings help them to keep their fingers on the pulse, keep a focus on what's really important, provide guidance as to any necessary changes and improvements.

It's important to stop and check if our customers see us as professional, high-end or bargain basement, cheap and cheerful. Is that how we want to be regarded? Different businesses will have different messages and criteria that they're keen to convey to their customers.

Let's look at some of the things it's important to consider from the start:

- Business literature may be the first introduction that some people have to your business. They may be handed a business card, leaflet or flyer or they may see an advertising poster offering goods for sale or the date of a seminar or workshop you're offering. What impression does it convey, how professional do you appear? Consider your branding and check if it's consistent throughout. Business cards often benefit from being good quality, especially as they may need to survive being stuffed into someone's pocket or purse alongside a handful of other people's.

  A professional impression is given when your stationery, articles and handouts contain relevant information so that customers can readily follow-up with you whenever they need. Keep your message clear and specific, especially if it needs to separately target several different niches and demographics to reach a varied customer base. It's important to tailor your message appropriately, whilst not forgetting to occasionally introduce new products, topics or services.

- Some people meet through network meetings. They're an effective way to identify people in business with whom you are looking to make new contacts. A good first impression can be made when you're interested in listening to what new acquaintances have to say. Identify what they're looking for, any problems they may be facing and see if there are ways you can help. Even if you can't directly resolve their problem you may know someone who can, which is a great way to establish a reputation as an important point of contact.

- What impression do your premises convey? It may be feasible to have your business premises in a rundown, inexpensive part of town, which helps keep your overheads down and is an effective way of appearing inconspicuous and low-key. However, might there be times when it's worth renting a more convivial business environment, e.g. for client meetings?

  If your customers and clients regularly call at your premises it's important to intermittently check on their experience and the impression they receive. Pretend to be your own customer occasionally. What does the area look like? How about your premises; are they shabby or smart? Would they benefit from a coat of paint, a good clean, some greenery growing in planters? Is there safe car parking, a friendly reception area? Some potential clients may decide to check on your place of work first, prior to booking an appointment or doing business with you.

- And last but not least, what about you, how do you present yourself as the face of your business? It may be that in working for yourself you rarely need to display a corporate image or be especially smart or well turned out, but research has proven that we all unconsciously assess someone within seconds of first meeting. Okay, a business suit or tie may not be necessary, particularly if you work from home but for many potential customers and clients looking professional goes a long way towards making a good impression. It demonstrates that you take your business seriously, care about how you present yourself and respect the people with whom you come into contact.

The saying 'we only get one chance to make to make a first impression' is very apt. There are many ways we can influence a potential customer and being mindful to create a good first impression is a positive start to affecting a successful outcome for all concerned.

Good Relationships Make Good Business Sense

Many of us appreciate the importance of being polite to others, of treating others as we would like to be treated but what about the ongoing implications of taking the time and making the effort to build good relationships. Let's look at how good relationships make good business sense.

Build good relationships in business. Networking, meeting and mixing with other people in business benefits us in many different ways. Firstly, from a purely practical point of view, meeting other business owners provides the opportunity for conversation and discussion, sharing information and advice, problem solving and providing mutual support. We may gain access to their contacts, both personal and professional, some of whom may be useful to us in any number of ways.

In addition we gain access to their knowledge, skills and expertise, which may help us develop personally and within our business. Access to other professions may provide help with business coaching, stress management, printing, graphic design, technical support, accountancy skills, insurance, all of which enable us to become more confident, strong and viable as a successful small business owner.

Meeting people in other businesses offers the opportunity to both utilise and recommend their services. Plus there's the possibility of establishing alliances where we can include our joint skills on the menu, extending our range of goods and/or services to provide a more comprehensive service to our combined clients.

With this in mind, it's important to nurture these relationships, follow each other on social media, meet up for coffee, keep in touch, treat each other well and get to know, like and trust each other. Remember discussions you've had and follow-up on them. Demonstrate genuine interest. Relationships and networking are not just about collecting stacks of business cards and then relentlessly bombarding each other with sales information. Maybe send out regular newsletters with interesting facts and articles that will be of help in their daily life. Be generous in recommending others, even if there's no apparent immediate payback to yourself.

Build good relationships with family and friends. Devoting time to your important personal relationships demonstrates to them and to you that they matter, that you care enough about them to commit time to doing things together. Being respectful of those relationships ensures that you have a strong, loving, supportive network in your life. These are the people who will try to understand and make allowances for you if at times you are under pressure at work, are stressed or have less time available for them on occasion.

These are also the people who can bring balance into your life, maybe at times tell you if you're wrong, over-doing things, damaging your health. They may not always fully appreciate your priorities or the demands that are placed on you, but family are for many people, a significant part of the reason why they are motivated to work as hard as they do.

Open and honest communications are an important part of personal relationships, of building a happy and secure home and personal life. Learn to say how you feel, share bad news as well as good, listen and be interested in others too. Relationships are a two-way exchange. It's equally important to do things you want to do, not just accommodate others and their wishes. Enjoy your relationships with family and friends and let them support you in your business.

Build a good relationship with yourself. So often we consider ourselves last, regard personal time and interests as something we may fit in after everything else on the list has been ticked. But personal time is great for de-stressing, for feeling valuable, for supporting your own self-esteem. Enjoying the things you really want to do makes the hours spent at work slaving over your computer, an order or a piece of work worthwhile. It's your personal reward for all the effort.

Some people even suggest that you should book yourself regular time in the diary and honour that time just as you would an appointment with an important client. Allowing an hour to read a book, take a leisurely bath, have a massage or go for a walk can make all the difference to your mind-set and feeling of wellbeing.

Certainly it's important to look after your health too. Take time to eat healthily, have regular breaks, aim to finish your work and domestic chores at a reasonable time, commit to quality sleep. But fun is also an important part of building a good relationship with yourself, of feeling worthy, that you're worth it, are entitled to consideration. Enjoy occasional rewards and treats as well as committing regular time for the things you enjoy, that add value to your life.

Ways to Encourage Your Customers to Buy

Whilst shopping is meant to be a pleasant experience very few of us appreciate being sold to. Many of us will have experienced being harassed by an over-enthusiastic sales person only to make our excuses, leave and purchase the very same item half an hour later in a more conducive environment.

It's good to buy but not so good to be desperately sold to. Similarly, when our customers reach their own decision to buy rather have us try to second-guess their needs it makes for a more pleasant experience all round.

Let's reflect on some effective ways to inform and persuade your customers and clients that trading with you is a positive decision; let's consider ways to encourage your customers to buy your goods or services.

- **Let them see you as an expert** who's happy to dispense advice, support and tips for free. Be genuinely keen to help your customers succeed; after all, that's a win/win situation for all concerned. When you demonstrate enthusiasm for what you do, show that you're not in it solely for the money you may even establish sufficient trust for them to be so confident in your advice that they make purchases based on your recommendation.

- **Don't appear too keen or desperate** to make a sale. Show that you're prepared to walk away rather than appear over-zealous about them making up their mind. Doing this removes the pressure and allows them to make up their mind in a calm, clearer way. They may even leave, reflect and return another day to make that very same purchase.

- **Be receptive to building relationships** and connections with other related businesses in order to expand your offerings to your joint client base. Doing this expands your customer/client reach, allows you to recommend and be recommended, so increasing your visibility. By establishing a reliable network of other businesses you can become an invaluable point of contact, the 'go-to' guy frequently in people's minds.

- **Use vouchers, offers and incentives** as a reward for loyal customers. Keep them informed of any special events, launches or training sessions you may be running. Include a 'use by' date to focus their minds. Articles, newsletters and mailing lists are an effective way of keeping your business fresh in people's minds and are a relaxed way of introducing new staff members, different skills and your full range of products and services over a gradual time scale. Existing clients need to feel important, be treated well and courted so they remain loyal to your business.

- **Don't forget the power of the last item on the shelf!** When there is one single, last remaining item on the shelf it can be a major inducement for customers to buy. The fear of running out of something that might be needed in the future can encourage an uncertain purchaser into immediately making up their mind.

- **It's okay if someone doesn't buy today.** It demonstrates great integrity to tell a potential customer that your goods or services are not what they're looking for on this occasion. This level of confidence can establish a relationship of trust where the customer is more than happy to return another time. Respect and honesty are important in maintaining a successful long-term relationship.

It's often said that people like to buy from people not from companies. When we feel comfortable with someone, like and trust them, we're happy to give them our business and recommend them to our friends and family members. Remembering these key points can ensure that old and new customers and clients choose you rather than your rivals and competitors.

Tips for Going the Extra Mile, Competing With the Big Guys in Business

As a small business owner it's important to be prepared to go the extra mile in business. The self-employed and small business owner can find significant ways to gain an advantage over medium or larger businesses, the big guys who may be tied to a specific range of goods and services, catchment areas or opening hours.

By being flexible and less rigid in their offerings the self-employed and smaller business owner may well be able to provide a more adaptive, tailor-made service to their customers and clients.

Let's look at some ways you could go the extra mile in business:

- **Anticipate your customers' needs**. I was impressed the other day when my accountant phoned me to make an appointment to call round and complete my annual tax return. Typically, I hadn't even begun to look at it and, like many people, dread it, often leaving it until the last-minute. I appreciated my accountant being on the ball, giving me the nudge to do something that needed to be done, and sooner rather than later. Personal service like this, anticipating what needs to be done via a familiar, recognised point of contact establishes good relationships with your clients and customers.

- **Say 'no' if something is not within your area of expertise**. It takes courage to decline business but it demonstrates integrity and respect for your own reputation and your customer's needs to be prepared to say 'no' to work that you cannot do to a satisfactory standard. Going the extra mile means staying true to your promise to do the best you can for your clients. If you take on work and then have to try to bluff your way through it can cause frustration and resentment in both you and your client as you both want the delivery of your usual high level of customer service.

- **Be willing to recommend** customers and clients to other businesses and providers who may, in certain circumstances, be able to deliver a better quality job than you. Going the extra mile means being committed to consistently providing the best workmanship by whatever means. Doing this enables you to establish yourself as a person of character and integrity. Bringing other businesses on board may result in you cultivating relationships and being able to deliver a wider range of goods and services, enabling you all to grow and become more successful.

- **Provide freebies**. Providing quality literature, workshops, seminars and networking opportunities allows you to keep in regular touch with your customers and clients, introduce them to any new innovations and changes in your business and educate them about your industry. You establish yourself as an expert, someone who's generous and supportive of your customers, who's prepared to go the extra mile.

- **Introduce your customers and clients to each other** if you think there's an opportunity for them to form meaningful business relationships. By supporting your customers to grow and become more successful you help them to strengthen and improve their businesses; you all benefit as a consequence.

- **Be honest if things go wrong** or if you've made a mistake. Most people accept that mistakes happen occasionally. Being honest about what's happened allows your customers to plan or make adjustments if necessary. Equally, be open and honest about timings, deadlines and costs. It lets your customers know what to expect, what they're dealing with and as such, plan around it. Again, integrity, honesty and mutual respect are important when you're going the extra mile in business.

Thinking outside the box, anticipating your customers' needs, being prepared to deliver exemplary customer service can set you apart from your competition and ensure that your customers continue to seek you out. Going that extra mile maintains your excellent reputation and continues to support your business success, even when competing with the big guys.

Is Your Business Partner a Bully?

No doubt, it seemed like a good idea at time! You met someone with skills complementary to your own. It seemed like a perfect fit, sharing the same goals, business ethos, enthusiasm for the future. Working together made perfect sense in a 'let's pool our resources, share overheads and motivate each other to success' kind of way.

Then reality starts to set in. You gradually come to realise that (s)he is aggressive, they make it obvious that they think you can't succeed without them and regard any good ideas as being theirs. At this point you may be tied financially, creatively and even contractually to them.

Let's identify the initial warning signs. A bully is often self-absorbed; they behave badly, keep their own hours, come and go as they please and often regard good manners as a sign of weakness. Over time their behaviour causes increasing stress and tension in the workplace, which may result in losing excellent staff who'd rather leave a well-paid job than work in an unpleasant environment.

Let's look at some tips for managing a bullying business partner:

- **Start by documenting examples** of their behaviour as they occur. Keep a diary log of times when they arrive late or leave early, are rude to staff or behave in an unprofessional or unacceptable way. This way you are able to provide factual evidence of times and dates which support your claims about their bullying behaviour. It may seem petty or trivial practice at the time but it's important to have evidence which supports your claims.

- **Become more assertive**. Bullies rely on people being afraid of them. They tend to shout louder and become more aggressive when they realise that their victim is intimidated by them. But when a bully meets their match, meets someone who is not afraid to stand up to them they often back down and become charm personified. Maybe consider hypnotherapy as a way of improving your confidence and self-esteem in order to become more assertive and able to stand your ground. Refuse to be intimidated, learn to speak your mind and become more adept at managing your business partner when he or she behaves badly.

- **Take regular breaks**. Bullies gradually wear people down by making the atmosphere increasingly stressful and negative. Over time their victims can become jaded, miserable and downtrodden. Start to take a break every ninety minutes or so and go for a walk outside, have a healthy snack, sit in the car for ten minutes and listen to some pleasant music. Detach from the atmosphere and you'll find that you return to work feeling re-energised and better able to manage the situation.

- **Have fun away from work.** Make sure that the other areas of your life provide a break which is satisfying and fun. Whether it be exercise, sport, a hobby, family or friends it's important to ensure that there is an area of your life which provides positive feedback and support.

- **Look after yourself.** Often a stressful, bullying atmosphere can be hard to switch off from and can be constantly on your mind. It can affect your sleeping and impact on the way you take care of yourself. Remain committed to looking after yourself.

  It's especially important in difficult situations to manage stress, follow a healthy diet, exercise, cut back on caffeine, alcohol and other stimulants and try to sleep regularly. Commit to finishing work and having some quiet time before bed. Maybe go for a swim or a walk, have a shower or a relaxing bath to symbolically wash away the day's cares.

- **Find an ally,** someone to talk to who provides reassurance that you are good, capable and going to be fine. Whether it be a friend or partner who will listen to you venting, or someone in a more professional capacity, like a business colleague or therapist, determine to get the support you need at this time.

- **Consider a Plan B.** What happens if this situation becomes completely unworkable? How long are you prepared to spend in this negative, destructive environment? Drawing up a Plan B can help to clarify your thoughts, reassess your skills and abilities and maybe find alternative ways to earn a living or branch out into something new, happier and more positive. Even if you chose not to implement it straight away, having a Plan B can provide light at the end of the tunnel. It provides the best mental approach for managing your business partner when you discover that he or she is a bully.

Tips for a Young Person's First Days at Work

Many young people will have now finished their education and be looking for full-time employment. Some will be in paid work from day one whilst others may start with being minimally paid as they begin their training as an apprentice or intern. Wherever they're working, the first days in a new job can be daunting.

Here are some tips to help on those important first days:

- **Ensure that on your first day you're punctual**; not too early and of course, not late. Either situation can throw your co-workers' plans for receiving you into disarray.

- **Locate the amenities** so that you feel confident about the logistics of the place. Find out the basics, where the rest rooms are, the coffee-making facilities, kitchen or cafeteria.

- **Smile** and be prepared to make the drinks, at least at first. Regard it as a friendly opportunity to meet everyone, learn their names and let them know who you are.

- **A nice touch** can be to bring in a packet of quality biscuits to let everyone share and enjoy during your first coffee break. It doesn't cost much financially yet can be another great way to say 'hello'.

- **Make an effort to quickly learn** your work email address, people's names, job titles, where everyone's located.

- **Make notes as you learn**. Hand-write the information so that you're able to readily access it. Highlighting important points may sound low-tech, but it's an efficient way to quickly identify key, relevant information.

- **What about mistakes?** There will be times when you don't understand something, make a mistake or are confused. Resist the temptation to bluff your way through. This option only serves to cause you stress and worry, annoys others and makes the situation far worse. Admit how you're feeling in an open and honest way, ask for extra instruction or clarification and focus on doing better in the future.

- **Be willing and keen but not desperate to please**. It's great to show enthusiasm but be wary about accepting too much responsibility before you fully understand what's entailed. Don't be in too much of a rush to commit to one particular role. Use this opportunity to take your time and learn about the company, the different roles and departments, whilst you have the chance.

- **Keep your own counsel**. Take time to assess the office dynamics before deciding who to befriend. Resist the temptation to criticize or complain about your work or other co-workers and managers. Others may have what they feel are valid grievances that they wish to share but you need to avoid being seen as a negative or disruptive addition to the team.

- **Focus on treating yourself well**. A new job is the start of a brand new phase in your life. It can be a tiring, stressful time. Ensure that you eat healthily, take breaks, have exercise and look after yourself by getting enough sleep. Give yourself rewards and treats from time to time.

Starting a new job can be stressful at any age. For a young person the first few days of a new job often means entering the alien, unfamiliar world of career development and business. And if you begin to realise that your first job situation, your first career choice is not for you, that's fine too.

Communicate your concerns to a mentor, a family member or responsible friend and help to get a clearer perspective on what your options may be at this time. It's early days in your business life; if necessary, you can start over. Hopefully some of these tips will help to ease the stress and support your transition to a successful working life.

Get Back on Your Feet After Being Made Redundant

Many people experience being made redundant at some point in their working life and yet, despite it being so prevalent, when it happens to us it can still hit us very hard. The very word redundancy is redolent of rejection, being discarded, of no longer having anything useful to offer. As a consequence, our reaction to it can affect many areas of our lives.

There are several ways to manage the stress, to cope better and start afresh:

- **The first thing to accept** is that redundancy is rarely about us or our capabilities and competency. Many companies have to release valuable staff as part of cost-cutting exercises. It's not uncommon for some staff to be later rehired as consultants, working on an ad hoc basis in a self-employed capacity. Being made redundant can sometimes open new doors and provide the potential for a viable new career.

- **The personal impact** of redundancy is often devastating. Confidence and self-belief can be seriously affected. We may feel too ashamed to tell family or friends at first, feeling embarrassed that we have let them down. The stress of being out of work, of having to find another job can impact on our health, stress levels, libido and ability to sleep.

Some people gradually find that redundancy prompts them to make changes to their life and career that they would never have otherwise considered. They decide to retrain in a completely different field, choose to turn a hobby into a business, decide to do something more fulfilling like charity work, re-evaluate their life or elect to get out of the rat race. It's not uncommon for people to say some years later that being made redundant was the best thing that happened to them. It forced them into making changes that improved their quality of life immeasurably.

Sometimes though, people may need a little help to reach that positive state of mind and hypnotherapy is one option that can improve a person's perspective and sense of worth. It can help a person cope better by reducing stress levels, feeling more confident and enabling them to start seeing themselves in a more positive way.

By visualising themselves as positive and successful they begin to feel more optimistic, exude better self-esteem and become more receptive to the opportunities that come their way. Hypnotherapy techniques can help at interviews and presentations; they can help a person remain calm and keep a clearer mind-set, focussing on a good outcome in whatever they're doing.

- **Home** is another significant area that can be affected by redundancy. Even if we receive a good financial settlement there's often still a requirement to maintain an ongoing source of income, particularly if there are children or only the one wage coming in. When we learn to feel calmer, less stressed about our situation we're often able to cope better, discuss appropriate ways to manage the situation and, as a result, interact more positively with other family members.

  Also, it can be all too easy to get into bad habits at home, to start to take our frustrations out on our partners or children, to become depressed and hang around all day watching television. It's important to remain proactive and use the time well, to get up, get washed and dressed each day, to continue to take good care of ourselves. This helps us remain better humoured, with a more positive, hopeful outlook.

- **Friends** can be an area where we struggle, perhaps through feeling embarrassed. We may feel too ashamed to see them, be concerned at spending money on socializing or feel reticent at admitting that we have not yet found another job. Friends may make suggestions that they regard as helpful but which are not appropriate for us, or they may be insensitive and fail to appreciate our level of distress.

We may need to find ways to improve our resilience and self-esteem, to learn not to take things personally and begin to appreciate our friends and their points of view. This may enable us to feel confident enough to cope with the stress of what other people think, to start to honestly explain our feelings, stay true to ourselves and be able to still enjoy a modified social life. Feeling more positive can help us to perhaps accept a little help and acknowledge the support friends offer without feeling embarrassed or guilty.

Redundancy can be a valuable time for a fresh start, to perhaps consider doing things at this time in our lives that we may not have given much thought to in the past. Many people use redundancy as a time to re-train, to start anew, to try things they may not have otherwise entertained. It can provide an opportunity for a positive new beginning at the next stage of life.

Make Retirement a Positive Experience

When we are young retirement can seem to be a distant notion, associated with old age, grandparents snoozing in their arm chairs and hours of daytime TV. The reality is that people are fitter than ever before, with great plans for their later years, enjoying lots of drive, determination and enthusiasm. They are using their retirement years in exciting and innovative ways. It's often a time when they catch up on doing the things they were unable to do in their earlier years.

Let's look at some ways to make retirement a positive time in life:

- **Financial planning** is crucial. Many people saved for their retirement through private or company pension schemes, but many of those schemes have been proven to be less than satisfactory. An increasing number of older people are supplementing their retirement income through part-time work. This can provide unexpected benefits; new interests, motivation and challenges, a regular routine that needs to be followed, the requirement to take care of one's appearance and the potential to make new friends in a more relaxing environment than was provided by a career-driven job.

- **Down-sizing one's home** can be an important consideration. Many retirement apartments provide a way to maintain independent living whilst introducing close proximity to other like-minded people. If family have left home, down-sizing can be a good way to reduce overheads and perhaps release some capital.

It's often a good idea to move whilst still fit and active as this is the best time to get to know new neighbours, form relationships and friendships and become an active member of the community. There's often access to a calendar of regular social activities and a guest bedroom which can be available for a nominal fee whenever overnight visitors come to stay.

- **Commit to looking attractive**. Feeling confident in one's appearance helps keep a positive, viable attitude alive; continue to dress smartly and remain in touch with fashion trends, colour and make-up. It's important to update one's look from time to time or else it may start to feel dated and stale. Wearing appropriate, fashionable clothing keeps a person looking good and improves personal confidence.

- **Keep up to date** with popular culture. Pay attention to the news, the latest technology, listen to modern music, watch the popular television programmes that everyone's talking about. Keep an interest in present-day life, even if you don't actively pursue every new fashion or trend. This choice maintains a regular participation in modern life and stops you feeling left behind.

- **Social activities** are aplenty for the over 50s and are often reasonably priced. Many Local Authorities provide exercise classes, swimming sessions, walking groups or table tennis, with refreshments often included. A regular weekly commitment means meeting the same people and them gradually becoming familiar faces to smile and share small talk with. This is a good way of making new relationships and doing things in a supportive environment. Over time these relationships could evolve into more by perhaps suggesting meeting for a coffee or going out for lunch.

- **Be proactive**. If there's nothing available in your vicinity why not set up some activities that might appeal to others. Encourage friends and neighbours to join you for a short walk once a week, arrange to meet for coffee or a game of cards at each other's houses, set up a singing group or choir, diary in a book club or games night. These activities have been known to blossom into eagerly anticipated, fun arrangements. All it takes is one person with a little drive and enthusiasm to start the ball rolling.

- **Consider further education** or hobby/interest classes. Was there a subject that you were really interested in but never had the time or money to study? My mother took up whist, tai chi, Egyptology and learned to play bridge, all at 81. Retirement can provide the opportunity to spend time on the subjects that interest you, and the beauty is that you don't need to take any exams unless you want to.

Every age in life has its advantages and disadvantages. Committing to a positive retirement can require a little planning as well as doing one's best to take care of one's health and finances. By being receptive to the viable opportunities and invitations that come along there is the potential for many satisfying and fulfilling relationships and activities to be enjoyed. These are all positive ways to improve your health, happiness and quality of life.

CHAPTER THREE

Stress and Relationships

The Best Way to Have a Great Relationship

There are two separate times in the year when divorce lawyers ready themselves for an influx of new clients; one of those is the post-Christmas fallout and the other is post-holidays. Both are times when people have typically been hot-housed together, anticipating fun, relaxation and shared jollity.

The reality is often very different, with the full-on stress and pressure of other people, children, conflicting wishes, excessive expenditure and even the weather causing well-intentioned plans to go awry. Good humour can start to fade, tempers often begin to flare and any flaws in the relationship can become highlighted.

Let's consider ways to reduce the pressure and improve our time with our special someone:

- **Be prepared to communicate**. Communication is not just about issuing instructions on what time the children need picking up or requesting some milk be collected on the way home. Take time to share each other's news, thoughts, feelings, fears and concerns. I've come across several relationships where one person has lost touch with what's happening at home or has no idea what their partner or children are doing on a day-to-day basis. Keep up-to-date, be genuinely curious about each other's lives and make time to talk about the personal stuff too.

- **Be happy to listen** and ask questions. Remember what's been said and follow-up on it afterwards. This shows that you want to be included and are keen to know more. Establish an ongoing conversation with your partner about them and their life. That way you both feel involved and supported.

- **Schedule proper quality time** to be with each other and demonstrate that it's important to you. Have fun and enjoy each other's company. Shower, dress up and look nice. By making an effort you prove you care, even if it's just for a simple dinner date at home.

- **Be loyal**. When one person is criticized or not supported by their partner in public, even as a 'joke' it can cause tension. They may feel ridiculed, mocked and disrespected. Other people may pick up on the subtle nuances of the comment which could influence their opinion of him or her. Being loyal means standing together in public, even if time does need to be set aside at a future date for a private conversation about serious or contentious matters.

- **Empathise**. It can be tough appreciating that the other person has a valid point of view, especially if we can't understand how they can possibly hold that stance! Respect them enough to agree to disagree rather than nag, bludgeon or try to force them to change their mind. There is a saying 'you may win the battle but lose the war'. Pick your battles and allow your partner to have their own opinions unless you feel it's too important to gloss over.

Equally, accept that sometimes your partner may feel they have a valid issue with you and your behaviour, just as you may have with them. Try to empathise and understand how it is for them, rather than become defensive or hostile. Establishing a great relationship means sometimes accepting that our partner may need to say if they're unhappy with us. It's important to be calm and receptive, prepared to discuss this in an adult fashion, whilst also becoming aware if they try too often to 'improve' us or 'remedy our failings', 'for our own good'!

- **Keep your own identity**. A great relationship provides companionship; it allows you to share closeness and intimacy, enjoy pleasing each other and doing things together. But it's also important to keep your own identity and not lose yourself in a relationship. Enjoy the security of your relationship as a place where you can improve your confidence and grow and develop as a person, becoming stronger over the years.

- **Be generous** and do things you don't want to do sometimes. There may be occasions with the in-laws or an event at work where your partner would value your support. You may not need to attend everything, but being supportive means turning up when it's important, with a good grace and a ready smile.

- **Allow each other quiet time** occasionally. It's not disloyal for your partner to sometimes want to be alone and have some private, personal time. Don't take it as rejection. Accept that not everything's about you. Acknowledge that sometimes your other half may be stressed, have had a tough day or simply be feeling the need for a little space. Be prepared to understand and accommodate each other whenever possible.

A sense of humour, sensitivity and respect all help you continue to enjoy a great relationship.

Five Ways to Tell if You Are Loved

There are many different ways to tell if we are truly loved by our partner. It's often the small, subtle things though, that make the real difference rather than the grand, elaborate gestures. Natural, automatic actions can make the difference between us feeling truly loved, rather than wondering if our partner is merely going through the motions and paying lip service to the relationship.

Let's look at some important ways that demonstrate love:

- **Gifts** are an obvious indicator of how our partner feels about us. Remembering special events and significant dates can be an important part of acknowledging our relationship and many people do delight in receiving expensive, lavish gifts, but ultimately it's the thought that counts. When our partner brings home a book that we've expressed an interest in, or even a free flyer for a talk by a speaker we admire it's a clear signal that we're being thought about with affection even when we're not together.

- A personalised gift, like a framed collage or scrapbook of souvenirs from times shared throughout the relationship can mean so much; assimilating tickets, photos, a shell from our beach holiday or a leaf from a forest walk may cost little in terms of money, but the time, effort and thoughtfulness of such a gesture is a wonderful sign of being loved. Someone going to all that effort for us means far more than an expensive piece of jewellery or bottle of fragrance purchased as an afterthought from a high-end store.

- **Physical closeness** is important in a relationship, but love is not just about sexual intimacy. When we are in a loving relationship we automatically touch each other as we walk by. We may unthinkingly rest a hand on our partner's leg or arm or lay our head on their shoulder. These actions display a relaxed ease in being together and a comfortable acceptance of each other's presence. Equally, when a couple start to become estranged it often becomes apparent as the physical and emotional space between them grows. They may even be unaware that the physical distance between them has increased as they move further and further apart.

- **Verbal support** is an important way of telling if we are loved. Both giving and receiving unconditional support and praise demonstrates pride in each other, evident to those who are within earshot. We are loved, cared for and supported by our partner and vice versa; proud of each other and not embarrassed to show it. Verbal support and love can include sending a text message that simply says 'thinking of you' or a text kiss. Love is also conveyed when we receive a compliment about something specific, about something we have said, done or are wearing, rather than a more general ambiguous comment or remark.

- Having a partner who **wants to spend time with us** is an important way to tell if we are loved. Sometimes life makes unavoidable demands on the amount of time we have available for each other, but there are other times which are more flexible and can be negotiated with. When our partner decides not to work, perhaps occasionally declines arrangements with friends or obligations with family in order to spend time with us it allows us to feel loved, important to them and sure that they want to be with us.

- **Quietly doing things to be supportive** and make our life easier is another way our partner can show their love. Helping with chores, doing what needs to be done or starting without having to be asked are all ways that can help to relieve our stress and demonstrate support. Our partner benefits as a consequence, because by helping and ensuring that we feel respected and appreciated we feel less tired, stressed or taken for granted and consequently happier and more secure within the relationship.

Different Ways to Enhance Your Love

When we're first attracted to someone we pay attention to everything about them. We notice the things they like, the times they smile, the little things they say and do. Finding small gifts, tokens of our love and ways to demonstrate our affection are easy to do because we are so tuned into the other person, as indeed they are to us.

Over time the relationship may develop into something more serious and we may decide to commit and live together. And so our lives become more routine and concerned with day-to-day requirements as well as each other. This is not to say that the love diminishes, we still love each other. But life gets in the way as we fret over bills, worry about a demanding boss, have elderly parents to consider or children to manage.

How can we find spare time and energy to invest in our relationship when we scarcely have time for the basic things in life? Here are a few thoughts that might help.

- Arrange alternate sleepovers or baby-sitting duties with other parents. That way you get a night off at no cost, confident in the knowledge that the children are safe and being looked after. Even if you choose to stay in with a simple take-away supper and a film, you still get a precious night where the two of you can enjoy being yourselves as a couple.

- Think back to your favourite places when you first started dating. The beach, the forest or a park, somewhere you can go and perhaps take a picnic and spend a few hours. Even if you share the day with your children, it can be fun remembering those early times, and could be a fun day for all.

- Run a bath with scented candles, bubbles and warm towels. Add a glass of wine or a mug of hot chocolate. Either or both of you can enjoy spending half an hour relaxing after a busy day. Followed by a massage, bliss!

- Offer a shoulder rub or foot massage whilst watching TV. Touch is a special way of keeping connected with each other and is a great way to relieve stress as well as being a thoughtful gesture.

- Pictures and photographs are a very personal touch. Finding a special picture of a place of significance or having a personal photograph taken and framed can be a way of signifying how special the relationship is. Some professional photographers offer to take a beautiful, tasteful photograph of the lady, dressed sensuously, maybe in lingerie, which provides an intimate gift for her partner.

- Write a love letter and conceal it somewhere unexpected, like a jacket pocket or a briefcase. Write all the things you love about them, include the special memories and things you would like to share together. It can be wonderful to find a special letter in an unexpected place, like at work, in a meeting or on the train.

- Send a text message or phone home just to say 'I love you'. Just that, nothing else but 'thinking of you and I love you'.

- Locating something that would be appreciated by your partner is a very thoughtful act. Buying a book or some music that you know they would enjoy is kind and considerate, as is seeing details of a show or talk that would appeal. The thought is what matters most.

Expensive gestures can be fine, but something as simple as cooking the evening meal or collecting the dry cleaning can mean more than an expensive gift or flourish. Just giving our partner the night off whilst we take care of the children or do the chores can mean the world to our partner and result in them feeling especially loved and appreciative of us.

What's the Deal with Foreplay?

There's a joke where 'are you awake?' constitutes foreplay in some people's eyes. Some people expect that all they need to do is touch their partner and sex will automatically follow. Indeed that is often the difference between sex and making love. Sex can become the perfunctory act of letting off sexual steam but doesn't really make the other person feel closer or valued. It may not feel especially loving.

Both men and women can feel used in these situations. I know of several men who feel that their partner uses them just for sex. They have become a sex buddy and whilst that may have seemed great at first, indeed their friends may express envy at their no-strings sexual relationship, they themselves have started to feel dirty and resentful of the situation.

Let's look at why foreplay is so important:

- It establishes rapport between two people. Getting to know each other's bodies, enjoying touching, tasting, smelling, and enjoying each other's responses as they share intimacy is an important way of becoming familiar and more sexually compatible within a relationship. It can also improve confidence in other areas of the relationship, as foreplay can be a precursor to becoming more comfortable and feeling able to discuss areas that need to be addressed.

- Spending time with each other is important. Often in a busy life their only really personal time may be in the privacy of their bedroom. Some people are so tired that when they eventually fall into bed the thought of sex is exhausting. Time being intimate and sexy, without being sexual can be a special, fun and relaxing time.

- It can be comforting to know that sex doesn't always have to follow. Some of my clients are nervous of demonstrating any sign of intimacy towards their partner because it's always misinterpreted as a desire for sex. Sometimes all they want is a cuddle or a little intimacy, but they avoid being affectionate out of fear of giving the wrong signals. Consequently, the thought of sex can become a chore and dreaded as an outcome of any affectionate encounter. Learning to enjoy foreplay in its own right is important. Enjoying the appetizers but not needing to follow with the main course can sometimes be enough.

- It provides reassurance. When a couple are stressed and too tired for sex, foreplay can provide closeness and contact, the reassurance that they are still attractive and fancied by their partner. If one person does not want sex, foreplay can help to maintain intimacy between the couple. It's also a good way to alleviate tension and stress and can help a couple relax and sleep better.

- It can improve the quality of the sexual act. Learning new ways of pleasuring each other, being adventurous and trying different things, taking time with love-making allows the experience to last longer and become more exciting. It provides an opportunity to practice, discuss and introduce different ways of enjoying the sexual experience together.

- Not all foreplay has to be in the same place. Some people enjoy teasing, flirting and suggestively tantalising each other away from the bedroom. Flirting in public can be an exciting way of demonstrating that you still find each other attractive. And it can make the recipient feel special and confident in the relationship.

Foreplay has a valuable role in an adult intimate relationship. It can be a sexy way of playing, demonstrating that you fancy each other and find each other attractive, sometimes followed by making love or, on occasion, enough on its own. Either way, foreplay can be an important way of communicating and enhancing your relationship.

Five Ways to Improve Your Sex Life

Many people find that when they are in a committed long-term relationship their sex lives can, over time, become perfunctory, routine and habitual, with sex 'performed' at certain times and ways each week. However, all it takes is a little thought and effort to make a difference and begin to improve your sex life.

Here are some tips to help improve your intimate times together:

- **Nurture your relationship**. Continue to work at your relationship by being loyal and supportive, demonstrate an interest in the things they like and show that you care about their well-being, happiness and satisfaction. When two people like each other they enjoy giving each other pleasure, a fun time and a satisfying experience. Consideration, mutual respect and concern can enhance the sexual experience for both of you.

- **Have fun**. Sex can be a serious matter but it should also be fun. Your sex life may well be improved by being a little less inhibited. Why not spend time sensitively exploring your fantasies together; role play, dress up, shop for toys and maybe watch a little pornography. Respectfully discuss what you'd both like to try, and then commit to experimenting with some of those suggestions. Perhaps take turns to offer ideas. A little encouragement may well help your partner gain in confidence and reveal his/her thoughts and fantasies, once they feel that it's safe, fun and acceptable to do so.

- **Share information** about your body; what you like and don't like. Get to know your body, how it responds, what works for you and what doesn't. Share that information verbally, by physically guiding your partner or by moving to communicate how you're feeling; share what you like and what you don't.

- **Relax** and agree that not every intimate encounter has to lead to full sexual intercourse. Sometimes we may be tired, stressed or simply not in the mood for full-on sex. Intimacy can also be about cuddling, touching and petting each other and that can be wonderfully enough. Sometimes sharing a bath, cooking their favourite food, giving each other a massage or snuggling up together and watching television can provide lovely intimate moments.

- **Flirting** with each other can be fun as well as another way to improve your sex life. Being sexy when you're out for an evening, playful or perhaps even a little provocative can build up sexual tension, excitement and remind you both of the chemistry and sexual attraction that drew you together. Take care to look after yourself, to keep yourself fit, attractive and healthy, pay attention to your personal hygiene and dress with care; all these are ways to ensure that you continue to fancy each other and find each other desirable sexually.

Many things can interfere with a healthy sex life; work pressures, the arrival of children or health issues can all cause our desire for sex to wane, if not to disappear completely. But a healthy sex life can strengthen the bond and continue to connect you and your partner in a very special way. It elevates your relationship from being simply a house share with a special friend into something far more intimate and meaningful.

When You've Got Something to Say, Say it Well

There are times in every relationship when it's important to communicate how we're feeling to our partner. We may have issues, annoyances, be upset, or there may be something of especial significance that needs a little time set aside to be discussed.

It can be tempting to second-guess how our words will be received and what the reaction will be. This can be compounded if we're feeling uneasy or apprehensive at voicing how we feel. It can escalate in our minds into a stressful conversation.

Feeling this way can put us at a disadvantage before we even open our mouths. It can cause tension and awkwardness to occur in our relationship. If we anticipate problems, setbacks and disapproval before anything has even been said it can cause us to regard the other person in a negative light. This view may have no bearing on reality, and yet over time can seriously influence the way we feel about the other person, potentially damaging the relationship.

So, let's look at the times when we really need to speak our mind in an effective way:

- When we anticipate trouble we prepare mentally in order to protect ourselves. That expectation will influence how we behave, the words we use, our tone of voice and our body language. When we're feeling a little nervous it's far better to try to remain calm, ask questions and uncover all the facts, rather than jump to conclusions and pre-empt what happens next.

- Focus on a good outcome and think positively about what it is that you want. When we say 'I don't suppose', 'I know I'm wasting my time asking' or 'you won't like this, but' we're setting the scene for a negative outcome. Many people don't realise how their words sound, what type of message they're unconsciously communicating or how they influence other people's perceptions. Gradually a positive or negative way of thinking becomes a habit. It's important to ensure that we develop good habits in our communication skills.

- From the outset determine to scatter positive suggestions and assumptions into your conversations. It sews the seeds for your success. Subtlety is the key. Referring to something that you want to receive/achieve/or expect to happen in a positive way can smooth the pathway to your desired outcome and remove the possibility of any other result.

- Be sure to present yourself well through your choice of words, your body language and tone of voice. You reinforce your message by nodding, smiling and accentuating all the positive benefits. Pause when you say something of particular significance and let your words take effect. Don't rush when speaking as that can indicate discomfort, embarrassment, uncertainty or a lack of confidence in what you're saying. By speaking slower you indicate that you're feeling calm, in control and happy to take your time.

- Be aware of any areas of dissent or controversy and be ready to appreciate the other person's point of view; be prepared to acknowledge those concerns. Have considered responses ready in case you're challenged, or you might even choose to deal with some of those points before they're raised. By doing this you demonstrate that you've given serious thought to what you want to say.

- Be prepared to give ground on things that are less important to you. Good negotiations include a readiness to compromise. If, for example, a young person wanted to go to a late night party a compromise might involve them agreeing to be dropped off or picked up afterwards at a particular time. This could result in their parents agreeing to transport them, the young person is allowed to attend the party and the parents are happy at knowing the address and their child's travel arrangements.

- Letting the other person claim credit for your good ideas can sometimes be a useful negotiation tactic. Guiding a discussion and interspersing ideas, hints or suggestions can sometimes result in those ideas being claimed by another person, as if they'd thought of them. You can smile, whilst getting what you want and allow them to feel good about their 'inspired' thinking. Being generous about the outcome allows everyone to enjoy a win/win result.

When we're clear about our wishes and are projecting ourselves in a positive way we show others that we feel confident and are taking responsibility for our own happiness and decisions. Everyone around us benefits when we're calm and assertive. We can overcome objections, sometimes in advance of them being raised. When we clarify our thoughts, overcome negative thinking and present ourselves as valuable, deserving and positive we're able to say what we've got to say in a constructive way.

Sorry can Sometimes be the Hardest Word

Many of us use the word 'sorry' frequently throughout the day. Even when we're innocent, when someone has bumped into us or has made a mistake, we're often quick to apologise and say 'sorry'. It's often an automatic response, said without thinking.

But what about the times when it really matters, when there is a genuine requirement for us to apologise sincerely for something that we have said or done, or not said or done. What happens then?

- Apologising can sometimes be regarded as a sign of weakness. We may be wary of admitting that we're in the wrong or are apprehensive at revealing an unfortunate side to ourselves. But usually saying 'sorry' is a positive decision to take. Many people feel respect for a person who has the confidence and integrity to hold their hand up, admit that they are in the wrong and apologise.

- Be genuine. There may be times when a direct approach is needed. The situation could not continue as it was. Be clear about what you're apologising for. You may feel regret at the way you handled yourself. Perhaps you could have been less confrontational or more sensitive and tactful. Saying 'sorry' for your lack of sensitivity or empathy may be the way forward, to prompt further discussion and to start healing the relationship.

- Avoid long explanations. There is nothing worse that someone starting to say 'sorry' who then launches into a long-winded explanation of how, when and why it all occurred. Sometimes brevity is important, especially if everyone is keen for the situation to move on.

- Sooner rather than later is best. Delaying making an apology can result in it seeming forced and insincere. Determining to put matters right straight away demonstrates a recognition of wrong-doing, a commitment to take responsibility and a desire to put things right.

- Difficult situations within families can sometimes be hard to apologise for. But if a parent has made a mistake or behaved badly towards a child it's important to show the child respect and apologise. Similarly, emotions can run high between in-laws or in a marriage. At times there can be an almost pantomime-like exchange, arguing who is right and who is wrong. A recognition that healing the relationship can sometimes be more valuable than winning the argument is important. Saying sorry and apologising is sometimes a gesture worth making.

- Actions speak loudest of all. When we have apologised it's important to prove that we meant what we said and that our words were honest and well-intentioned. Endeavouring to behave better and not repeat the same mistakes is important.

Interestingly many people find that when they make the first move and start to apologise the other person usually responds in a positive way. They are often so relieved that the difficulty and tension within the relationship appears to be coming to an end that they start to apologise too.

Tips for Effective Communications

We all communicate constantly throughout the day. A large proportion of communication is non-verbal, through body language and unthinking responses; a brief grunt, a shrug of the shoulders, a reactive scowl or unconscious smile can all convey a lot without us really being aware of how we're appearing to others.

Let's look at some useful tips to improve your communication skills:

- **Focus and really listen** to what the other person is saying. Be attentive to how they seem to be feeling. This requires being fully present with them, giving them your undiluted attention and being interested in what they have to say.

- **Show them that you are listening** by being responsive and contributing to the conversation, smiling and appearing relaxed. Some of the most effective communicators appear to have all the time in the world when they are deep in conversation. They make each person feel special, interesting and important. So ask valid, relevant questions. When we are interested in someone or something we want to know more. Asking questions allows the speaker to feel that you are completely absorbed.

- **Active listening** involves demonstrating that you have heard what's been said. By looking at the other person as they speak, nodding, waiting for them to finish and reflecting back some of what they have said to double-check that you have listened and correctly understood, you prove that you are interested and respectful of them and what they have to say.

- **Refer back** to what you have been told when next you meet. Building a relationship means establishing a connection, an ongoing awareness of each other's lives. When you share a conversation with someone you see regularly, remembering what you have been told allows them to feel important and of interest to you. Continuity allows a relationship to grow and become stronger, perhaps developing into something meaningful over time.

- **Be clear** as to what you want to say. When there's a sensitive matter to discuss or a difficult, conflict situation that needs addressing it's important to think before you speak. Decide what your issues or concerns are and what you feel you need to say. This allows you to start with a clear agenda and be able to keep on point.

- **Pick your moment**. Just because you have something important that you want to discuss doesn't mean that it's a good time for the other person. They may be tired, stressed or have other things on their mind. Wait until they're in a more receptive frame of mind, especially if you're looking to win them over.

- **If there's a difficult topic to discuss**, it's important to allow adequate time to discuss it properly. Arrange a mutually acceptable time so the conversation doesn't need to be rushed. Some people like to agree a code word in advance, one they can use it if they need a time-out due to feeling distressed or overwhelmed. It allows a short break during which they can calm down.

- **Avoid accusations**. Effective communications require a two-way exchange of ideas, thoughts and information. Accusations can introduce an attack and defence mind-set, where the conversation goes completely off point. I'm sure you're familiar with the 'I only said that because you' scenario. The use of examples and accusations can cause any discussion to dissolve into acrimonious bickering. Indeed, many couples find that this can become a regular pattern. Relationship counselling can help provide a more structured setting in which to explore issues, stay on track and allow for more meaningful communications.

- **Take responsibility for how you feel**. Rather than being accusatory towards the other person or expecting them to be psychic, it's far more effective to take responsibility and say how you feel. Then you can explain why you're upset about something. This approach will often prompt the other person into being more supportive, understanding and keen to help the situation resolve.

  Equally, taking responsibility helps to improve your confidence levels and find your voice rather than always trying to please others, avoid confrontation and not be a nuisance. Counselling and hypnotherapy can help to improve this situation with both offering positive ways to overcome past issues and enable you to express your feelings in a more constructive way.

- **Body language** is a giveaway. Leaning slightly towards the person who is speaking indicates an interest and involvement in the conversation. Face them and look at them as they speak. I had a friend who always used to place herself so that she could look past me to see who was entering the bar or restaurant whenever we went out socially. Disconcerting to say the least! I certainly didn't feel that she was interested in what I had to say.

- **Honesty and good manners** are an important part of effective communications. Being dishonest or pretending to agree or be interested may be a polite or appropriate response on occasion. But if you aim to establish a genuine, long-term relationship it's important to be truthful about your opinions and feelings. Good manners are about consideration of the other person's sensibilities. But for a relationship to be real there has to be integrity, honesty and respect.

The Stress of Starting to Date Again

Many of us will have had a variety of dating experiences. Starting with the early crushes at school and then the intensity of our first loves, we will no doubt have experienced many ups and downs throughout our dating life. As we get older we may decide to consider more seriously the importance of choosing wisely in order to form a successful relationship with a potential new life partner.

It may be useful at first to commit to dealing with our issues and address the reasons why previous relationships have not worked out. It can be valuable sometimes to take a break from dating and focus on ourselves, on healing unhelpful patterns, such as neediness, jealousy or possessiveness. Then we're able to work out what it is that we really want from a long-term partner and feel ready to start dating again.

Let's look at the best way to enjoy re-joining the dating game:

- **Be true to yourself.** Many people look to the press, popular magazines, their local clubs and bars to check out what it is that they 'ought' to be wearing. It can be fun to be aware of what's 'on trend', the latest fashions and popular places to go, but turning yourself into a clone of everyone else is no recipe for success in the dating game. Wearing clothes you're uncomfortable in and hanging out in places you don't enjoy can be wearing, draining and tiresome, especially if you'd much rather be doing something completely different. Being true to your interests, likes and dislikes is a much more effective way of finding someone suitable for you.

- **Appreciate advice** but make your own choices and decisions. The important people in your life, family and friends, are often keen to see you settled because they then don't have to worry about you being on your own. Obviously they want you to be happy, but may have their own agenda with advice and opinions.

Acknowledge their input and concern but remember that it's you who has to live with the choices you make. Take a step back and work out what's best for you.

- **Take care of yourself.** Previous hurtful relationships may have damaged you and impacted on your confidence and self-esteem. Taking a little time to refresh your image can pay dividends. Maybe take the opportunity to update your look, lose a little weight, tone up, revamp your wardrobe or learn some new skills. Making an effort to invest time and energy into yourself can prepare you to re-join the dating scene.

- **Say 'yes' to invitations.** Even something that does not sound especially appealing may lead to making new friends, spending time with interesting people or engaging in fun, unexpected activities. Say 'yes' because you never know where it may lead.

- **Maintain an interest in current affairs**, popular culture and local activities. It's useful to be able to join in with conversations and discussions, especially when you're looking to meet a new date. It's important to be able to enjoy easy chatter. Yes, conversing in a professional capacity may come easily to you. There are clear expectations and parameters in those situations. Social conversations can be more stressful as there is often no agenda. Keep up-to-date with the things that are of general interest, then you can feel confident about initiating or joining relaxed conversations.

- **Be proactive** with your social life. Familiarise yourself with details of interesting events, concerts, shows or sporting fixtures and organise outings with people in your group. This way you keep busy, have a fun and interesting time away from work and maybe even meet someone with whom you get on especially well.

Having a special someone in your life adds companionship, support, friendship and even sex into your life. Being out of the dating loop for a while can impact on your self-esteem, confidence and create a rather unsettled feeling. Whilst going through this phase it's important to look after yourself and appreciate the single life. Then when you do find someone you want to date you'll be in a good place, rather than desperate to find anyone who's ready to fill the 'job vacancy' of boyfriend or girlfriend. Be prepared to wait for someone who will enhance your life and make you happy.

Meeting a New Date Online

Some people still remain a little cautious about meeting a new date online, and it's indeed important to be careful about how much information you reveal about yourself, certainly at the outset. Other people may prefer the more traditional approach, saying that there's no substitute for the frisson of excitement and the chemistry you feel when you unexpectedly meet someone you're strongly attracted to.

But modern life has many stresses and pressures which limit our availability to go looking for a potential new partner. We don't all have the time or opportunity to be receptive to the people we encounter in our busy daily lives or to engineer new opportunities.

Meeting someone new can be very difficult when you're new to an area, working long hours, newly single or have limited time or money to socialise. Joining a dating site and meeting someone online can be a fast and effective way to get things started.

Let's consider some of the benefits of dating online:

- You cut out the randomness of keeping your fingers crossed and hoping that you'll meet the right person by chance. When you join a dating site you're able to specify what you're looking for and tailor your search criteria to your personal preferences. Musical tastes, age range, location, pet lover, smoker or non-smoker can all be specified; all the things you may take a long time to discover if you randomly met someone in person. Yes, you might be prepared to compromise and share their interests if there is real chemistry but important differences can become divisive and eventually make you incompatible. Going online can eliminate those situations.

- It's easy to share personal information relatively quickly, before you even meet, in an online relationship. You can get to know someone very well and feel that you've established a strong connection and friendship. Communicating online and sharing phone calls means that you have time to think about what you're going to discuss in advance. It's easier to reveal things that you may not have readily opened up about if you'd initially met face to face. Often people say that they feel comfortable volunteering details about themselves that they've never told anyone else before.

An online relationship progresses differently, as physical intimacy, touching, kissing and sex, or even seeing each other's body language, are not initially an option. It can mean that discussions become more in-depth than in the early days of a more traditional relationship. Effort is invested in having interesting conversations, sharing information, asking questions and demonstrating an interest in each other's story.

As the relationship progresses, both are keen to form a picture of what each other is like, to learn about each other's views and opinions and to share more than simple daily updates and gossip. Lighter conversations will occur too, but wanting to get to know someone online means being more focussed on spending time developing the relationship until such time as you both decide to meet.

- It's convenient to have introductions to potential dates delivered to your account and then be able to take time over your reply, sharing your thoughts and feelings from the comfort of your own home. If you met someone in person it would be highly unlikely that you would say, 'tell me about your childhood/home life/work/past relationships' and then remain silent whilst that happened. Doing this online, in private, at a time to suit allows each person to commit their full attention to each other's story.

Online dating is growing in popularity and is an efficient and effective way to meet a potential new partner in these fast-paced times. However, paying attention to personal safety is an important consideration, so it's essential to be cautious about revealing too much about yourself. Then, when going to meet each other for the first time it's important to implement some basic guidelines; after all, you only know what they've chosen to tell you online.

Go to the first date in your own car so that you can leave when you want. Agree to meet in a public place as it's safer. Set a time limit of an hour or two, in case either of you begin to feel uncomfortable or feel that there's no chemistry. Take your mobile phone with you and maybe have a friend call after an hour to check that you're okay. Trust your gut; if you feel uneasy or unsure pay attention to that instinct and don't agree to anything that doesn't feel right. Then, once your safeguards are in place, relax and enjoy the opportunity to go ahead and meet new dates and make new friends.

An Abusive Relationship Can Creep Up On You

Imagine you went on a first date with someone who was sarcastic, nasty or disparaging towards you. It's hard to believe that you would agree to a second date. Yet gradually we can find ourselves accepting that behaviour, justifying it and perhaps even feeling that we are in some way responsible for it happening.

The abuser often couches their behaviour subtly; they may claim they are trying to help us improve, are encouraging us to remedy a perceived failing or flaw and are doing it for our own good!

It is often sexual abuse that gains the most media coverage but the term 'abuse' also covers physical, emotional and mental cruelty and can be experienced by people of either gender, any age and in any strata of society. That's why it's important for us to notice if any escalating patterns of unacceptable, sustained bad treatment start to appear.

- **Abuse is often about control**. The abuser may be insecure, afraid of losing you or be fearful that you'll find someone better, so they try to hold onto the relationship by checking where you're going, what you're doing or how you're spending your money. They'll comment negatively on how you dress and even question and criticise whoever you're in communication with.

  Often an abuser will try to make you increasingly dependent and reliant on them. They may discourage you from working; they earn enough, why not take a break, why not take time to think about doing something else? It can be a seductive, attractive process, where you feel cared for, loved and supported, but over time you'll gradually lose your financial independence, career, friends and even family.

- **Emotional abuse** often starts by establishing a cosy 'us against the world' scenario where you're assured that you're all they have/need/want. At first you feel special and secure, safe in the loving bubble of warmth and protection. Gradually you'll find you spend less time with friends, especially if it becomes an increasing hassle to make arrangements, where they are referred to as a bad influence or your family is accused of being unfriendly or interfering. Sometimes friends or family may even be accused of inappropriate behaviour in an attempt to isolate you even further and so allow the controlling to continue.

Over time it can become harder to make plans to see 'outsiders'. You may find that when you do try to make plans they often clash with 'special' or 'important' functions that you're required to attend, or there is an insistence in dropping you off and picking you up, where your partner invariably returns earlier than agreed.

This in itself may be fine. You justify their behaviour as loving, attentive, friendly, sociable or helpful, but combined with negative remarks about your clothes, hair and makeup you may gradually start to lose any confidence in yourself.

Some abusers become so controlling that they methodically check every financial transaction and request for money, query every call or text on the itemised phone bill, undertake daily mileage checks on your car, monitor your social media or return home at unexpected times to see what you're doing. If you try to challenge their behaviour they will justify themselves in a logical and reasonable way, even making you feel guilty and apologetic for having questioned their motives.

- **Physical abuse** often starts with a tap, a push or an angry slap. Sometimes alcohol is involved. The perpetrator is often seriously contrite afterwards, promising never to repeat their behaviour. It's important to be firm with them and discuss what's happened from the outset. Insist that they seek help, perhaps to specifically deal with anger or alcohol-related issues. Keep a diary of abusive behaviour, try to save money in a secret account and locate a safe place where you know you can go if you become afraid of their behaviour.

However, if you find that you're becoming increasingly afraid it is definitely time to report his or her behaviour to the police and to social services if children are involved. Someone who starts to physically abuse you is likely to escalate their behaviour and in all likelihood the abuse will become more frequent and more severe as time passes.

- **Sexual abuse** can involve gradual but increasing degradation; the pressure to do things and engage in practices that you find off-putting, unpleasant, painful or humiliating. You may be accused of being frigid, a prude or old-fashioned but whilst it can be fun to experiment and explore sex together, a relationship should be about both parties feeling comfortable and moving at a pace that is fine for both of them.

'Start as you mean to go on' is an important message for new relationships. Keep regular channels of communication open between you and be sure to discuss any areas you feel unhappy about. Be firm and refuse to be bullied into doing things you don't want to do. You're allowed to change your mind even if you've gone along with things on previous occasions.

If you're beginning to feel uneasy in your relationship, find an ally with whom you can confidentially discuss matters. It may be that you're being over-sensitive, feeling vulnerable, or past experiences have made you ultra-cautious. Even if that is the case, you're still entitled to consideration and respect; it's valid that you have your concerns listened to. Might it help to find a place where you could go to de-stress and take a break, giving you both time to reflect on your relationship? Might you benefit from outside help from a counsellor, a mediator, priest or family friend?

Take time to explore what the triggers are, what happens to spark off your partner's abusive behaviour. Is alcohol a factor, does other people's flirtatious behaviour, perceived intelligence or influence over you exacerbate situations? Highlight what sparks off each episode and determine to find help for either or both of you to deal with those issues. It's important to protect yourself and your self-esteem, and as a consequence you may even spur your abuser to seek the help they need too.

Holidays Can Put a Strain on Your Relationship

Many people have high expectations of their holidays. They spend weeks, even months, hoping that everything will be blissful and idyllic. Reality can mean that things don't always go to plan, as they discover that they're not as relaxed with each other as they'd hoped and may have even grown apart from each other. Holidays can put one heck of a strain on your relationship!

It's interesting that whilst many family lawyers comment that New Year is often the busiest time for people to seek a divorce, after the full-on closeness, stress and drama of a family Christmas spent together, it's also a fact that holiday times and long bank holiday weekends can place an inordinate amount of strain on our relationship.

Consider how our normal day-to-day living consists of much familiar, automatic routine, of us being aware of our roles, of what's expected of us, having tasks that we regularly undertake before we collapse in front of the TV or wander off exhausted to bed.

Holidays can put any flaws or short-comings in our relationship under the spotlight as we book time away, expectantly hoping to have fun together and rekindle some of the old spark and intimacy during our trip.

Here are some tips that can help to ease the strain of holidays:

- A de-stress session before your holiday can be a good idea. I have clients who come for hypnotherapy so that they're able to relax immediately their holiday starts, rather than typically taking 2-3 days to wind down from their busy work schedule. A pre-holiday massage is another valuable way to reduce stress, strain and tension.

- Discuss in advance if there are specific things either of you would like to do during the holiday. Some people simply want to relax by the pool or on the beach. Others would hate to do that and prefer to explore, walk miles or browse through markets and sight-see. Discuss if you're happy to compromise and do a little of both or would prefer to spend some time enjoying things separately. This way any areas of potential strain are out in the open and have been talked through in advance.

- Some couples only realise when they're on holiday that they have lost the art of chatting conversationally with each other. They've stopped sharing banter and chit-chat and now simply exchange information and updates when they're at home. It may be a revelation to discover how far they've drifted apart and lost touch with each other's lives, interests, hopes and dreams.

  If this is you, then your holiday can be a good time to focus on what needs to be done; talking, taking time for intimacy and love-making and generally having fun together. It can be a great opportunity to sensitively discuss your relationship and agree on the importance of scheduling regular 'us' time as part of your post-holiday plans.

- Children often benefit from playing and spending time with other children whilst they're on holiday, as do their parents from having a little free time on their own. Check if you need to book children's clubs in advance and then aim to make the most of your personal time and spend it doing companionable things as a couple.

- If you're spending the holidays at home, try to ensure that some time is committed to fun activities and not just doing chores, DIY and projects around the house. Plan some leisurely time together for relaxing lunches, walks and catching up on idle conversation. Aim to reconnect and enjoy each other's company.

Holidays can provide an opportunity to put life's daily stresses and pressures to one side for a while. They're a time to interact with each other as the couple you used to be before life/children/work/stress got in the way. They can provide an opportunity to revisit what first attracted you to each other when you met, as well as time to reconnect with your relationship and remind yourselves of how good it could be once again.

Use the opportunity to relax, practice sensitivity, respect and commit to communicate well whilst letting go of some of your daily stresses and strains. Use your holiday as a time to refresh yourself and your relationship.

Tips for Dealing with an Anti-Social Partner

Sometimes we may be faced with a difficult situation with our partner. He or she may become increasingly anti-social or refuse to mix and meet with our friends or family. We may try to be supportive and understanding for a time but eventually we can become more and more frustrated with the situation. It can be hard to know what to do, how to handle times like this, especially if we're a sociable person who loves using free time to catch up with family and friends.

Let's look at some points to consider when our partner is becoming increasingly anti-social:

- At first, try to explore the reasons behind his or her behaviour. Could they be depressed or struggling with stress; might there be a problem that you're unaware of? Sometimes people retreat into themselves and become increasingly isolated when they feel out of their depth. The thought of being sociable, chatting and laughing animatedly with others can fill them with dread. Pay attention to their day-to-day behaviour and look for clues. Are they sleeping okay, how is their appetite, temper, sense of humour or libido? Changes in any of these areas can signify that there is more to this than them simply feeling anti-social. They may need to visit the family doctor for a health check-up or look at counselling or stress management therapy.

- Incorporate activities into your free time and holiday periods that your partner feels are of value. Some people feel that free time should be used for 'worthwhile' activities like tackling outstanding chores. Agree to spend half a day in the garden or tidying the garage. Then you can both feel that you've earned the lunch at a country pub with friends or going to see a film.

- If there is a backlog of chores that are getting them down, might it be worthwhile hiring someone else to help? If you can afford it, it can make sense to pay someone to do the cleaning, ironing or decorating so that you can spend your free time together relaxing and having fun. When a couple spend all their time working, they can lose sight of the friendship side of their relationship and life can become a little humdrum. Remind each other of what is important and commit to enjoying each other's company.

- Could there be other reasons for your partner's attitude towards your friends and family? If they feel uncomfortable with them might there be valid reasons for their feelings? Ask them the question and then wait for the reply. There's no point in second-guessing what's on your partner's mind.

  They may not like your behaviour when you're with your friends and family or be uncomfortable with their attitudes and idea of fun. Give your partner the opportunity to verbalise their feelings. Then you can discuss what options you both have to deal with the situation.

- Some people have very different views on how they like to spend their free time. For these people there can be two equally valid ways to resolve this dilemma. One is to take turns to decide on an activity and then participate together. This can bring new experiences into both your lives. The other is to spend some free time apart, each doing your own thing, after which you meet up to share the day's news and adventures. Whatever works best is the most appropriate option for you.

Let Children See Disharmony Resolved

In any family or relationship disharmony occurs on occasion. It's a fact of life that people will not agree on everything all of the time. All too often though, when a potential row seems to be brewing, children will either be asked to leave the room or the disagreement will be put to one side to be forgotten about or to be continued later, in private.

If this happens children may never learn about the process of resolving disagreements. All they will see will be the early stages of how a row begins, perhaps with niggling and tension. And then they will witness the after-effects, which are perhaps long cold silences, or everything suddenly becoming fine again because the air has been cleared.

Children need to appreciate that disagreement is an accepted part of life and that there's a useful talent in being able to navigate a row through to a satisfactory conclusion. Arguing can be done in a positive or a negative way. Teaching children about disagreeing with respect and how to then reach a satisfactory conclusion is one of the most important lessons in becoming a rounded, confident adult.

Let's look at three types of arguments:

- **Constructive arguments** are when issues are raised, talked through and then resolved. Everyone has their say, feels listened to and respected. After this, a satisfactory outcome is reached and everyone feels pleased about the process.

- **Productive arguments** are when issues are raised but are not always resolved. Often it can take a lot of courage to raise these issues, especially when another person's views are known or suspected to be very different to one's own. Raising matters and discussing them gives everyone an opportunity to discover how each other feels and hopefully attain a level of insight and understanding. A productive argument means that the discussions have been respectful and appreciative of each other, even if the participants then agree to disagree.

- **Destructive arguments** often include shouting, anger, loss of control and maybe even violence. These situations are often highly emotional with a lot of pent-up feelings being released. Often no one gets heard at these times and nothing gets resolved. There is too much going on to make much headway with these arguments.

Children sense when something is wrong. Being sensitive to atmosphere and underlying tension is part of our natural human survival instinct. So bringing problems into the open is a more honest way of acknowledging that something is wrong and then taking time to deal with it. Children find it easier when parents argue in front of them. They can make sense of it, rather than wonder and speculate about what is the matter, or worry if they are in some way to blame or responsible for any of the problems that are causing the disagreements.

It's more disturbing for children if their parents suddenly divorce after having had no apparent problems. In a way, arguing lets them know that all is not well. Then they can be a little more prepared if the situation does deteriorate into a breakup.

Teaching children about appropriate ways to argue and disagree is part of a child's education and preparation for later life. Then they learn about discussion, about not taking things personally and about listening and negotiation. All these skills are valuable qualities for interacting and forming successful relationships with others throughout life.

Do You Need to Take a Sabbatical From Your Relationship?

Every so often there is coverage in the media on the benefits of taking a break from your relationship. Having some timeout can provide a breathing space from the stress it may be causing you. It gives you the opportunity to reflect on your life, what your relationship means to you, to ponder the good and the bad and really consider what it is you want.

But are there other ways of reaching that same level of insight and awareness? Do you really need to take a sabbatical from your relationship to discover if it's right for you? Let's look at four C's that might influence whether or not you need to take a break from each other for a little while:

- **An ability to communicate.** Many couples struggle with communication. They lead exceptionally busy lives and have many demands on their time. Often, when they reach home there is still much to do, by way of chores, cooking and the demands of growing children. Taking time to converse properly with a partner can seem to require a massive effort, when all you want to do is soak in a relaxing bath or enjoy a glass of wine and watch TV. Many couples end up effectively house-sharing, where their main communication is 'we're out of cereal' or 'can you pick up the dry-cleaning'.

A sabbatical can provide an appealing escape from everyday life and its demands. It can mean that when you do meet up you schedule that time exclusively for your relationship; time to do pleasant things together and have adult conversations like you did way back at the start of your relationship. You discuss each other's days and share your thoughts and feelings.

In your day-to-day life today consider how you demonstrate the way you feel about your partner through your words and actions. Many people have successful relationships because they plan to include 'us' time in their lives. They delegate some of the mundane tasks to others in order to have space in their lives for each other. Would it be feasible to have a cleaner once a week, have your grocery shopping delivered, send out the ironing or give the children some tasks? What about having one evening a week where you freshen up, dress nicely and sit and eat dinner together with distractions like the television or phones switched off? Think of something that could work for you that provides an opportunity to focus on your relationship and support better communications.

- **A preparedness to compromise.** Many of us have relatives, friends, hobbies or jobs that our partner might not 'get' or might regard as more of a nuisance than a pleasure. These external demands can place a strain on a relationship, especially if there is an undercurrent of pressure and tension over the amount of time these interests consume. There might be a resultant feeling of not being respected or understood which could ultimately escalate into a need for a sabbatical in order to reflect on how the relationship is working out.

  Consider ways that time can be found to accommodate the things that both of you regard as important. Could you both pursue family/friend/work/hobby related interests separately and then meet up afterwards? Having separate interests can add interest and conversation to a relationship. There's no reason why you have to do everything together. If there are times when it's required to bring along a partner remember that compromise is about occasionally doing things you don't want to do in order to show support for your partner.

- **Look to co-operate.** Work together, even if there are things you disagree about in private, behind closed doors. Build a solid relationship and discover that your relationship works better when you act together as a team. Presenting a united front allows both of you to feel supported, strong and with a good friend and ally by your side. Loyalty can be an important part of this commitment. It means that whatever you both think in private, you co-operate and work together for the greater good.

  Co-operation also means that when one of you is overloaded the other steps in to provide extra help and support. There are times when one of you will be extra-supportive and other times when the roles may be reversed but no one keeps a tally, that's the way it works; it's about give and take.

- **Remember to connect.** Remaining aware of the various demands on your relationship allows you to discuss how you feel about those external demands and distractions. Having a strong connection means being honest with each other about how you feel, even if there's no apparent solution in sight. There may be issues with an impossible workload, a relative who's seriously ill or a friend who's going through a bad time and you or your partner feels they have to be involved.

Discuss how you feel, reassure each other that they're your top priority but that you need some latitude during this time. Demonstrate your love and try to allow regular quality time to meet and talk, to have a little fun, and enjoy a pleasant interlude together.

By treating your relationship as important, not taking each other for granted and maintaining an attitude of respect and openness you may find that your relationship remains consistently good. Then there may be no need to take a sabbatical from your relationship.

How to Spot the Signs That Your Relationship is Over

Sometimes there comes a point when we are dating or in a longer-term relationship where we have to face the facts and acknowledge that our relationship is over. We may try to bury our head in the sand, make excuses and pretend that it's not happening, but there comes a time when we have to admit that the other person is backing off and it's time to call it a day.

Let's look at some of the clues that can suggest your relationship is over:

- They avoid your calls. If someone is not answering your calls, not 'phoning back or is ignoring your texts then it's evident that they don't want to speak to you, don't know what to say and are trying to cool things off.

- They are working longer and longer hours. This can sometimes be difficult to quantify. Many people are required to work long hours and many people don't work standard office hours. There may be a requirement to justify their position, clear a backlog of work or satisfy a demanding boss or clients, but if someone is increasingly working longer and longer hours and is rarely available to see you, you must then decide if this is the relationship for you.

- They regularly include others in arrangements. When a couple are strongly attracted to each other they want to spend time together, be in each other's company and share things exclusively between them. If the relationship starts to feel strained or jaded they may try to include others in their activities as a way of causing a distraction or to dilute the intensity.

Explanations may sound reasonable and be hard to argue with: it will be more fun, others are interested in participating or it's more sociable to do things as a group. If it happens regularly it may be that the real reason is to avoid spending time together in close proximity. They may want to disengage from being part of a couple.

- They start to prefer spending time with other people or doing things that you don't enjoy. There may be a flurry of arrangements made without you being invited or consulted, or events arranged by others that your partner feels inclined to attend alone. Either way, it means that you are effectively becoming less important in your partner's diary.

- Body language becomes more distant and defensive when a relationship is coming to an end. The subtleties of smiling, touching, being relaxed and open with each other all start to change when one person is backing off from a relationship.

- Your partner doesn't laugh at your jokes anymore. All the little 'our' jokes, the personal, amusing anecdotes and references appear to be forgotten or are no longer remembered as funny or relevant. In fact they may appear to be regarded as irritating or foolish.

- Criticism becomes more evident. The united front and appreciation of each other's opinions that was so much a part of the relationship at the beginning is now no longer evident. Instead of defending you or understanding your viewpoint there is now an increased tendency to complain, admonish or be irritated by you.

- Intimacy from kissing, flirting and sexual contact all start to be avoided. Public displays of affection are neatly side-stepped as embarrassing or inappropriate. They are too tired for sex or personal demonstrations of love and affection when alone.

On their own, some of these signs may mean that your partner is stressed, worried or unhappy. There may need to be a gentle but serious conversation to discover what's going on in their life. However, if the relationship is over it's often better to talk it through, to discuss if it's retrievable, to decide if you're going to break up in a friendly way or at least end it with some dignity intact. No one benefits from fighting to retain a relationship if one person has fallen out of love and moved away emotionally.

Is it Time to End Our Relationship?

Recognising the time has come to end a serious relationship is often especially stressful. We may have shared many good and bad times together, grown up with them and certainly loved them for a time. We may even still love them, but not in the way we know we should.

But there can be a lot of distress, confusion and angst over ending a relationship; are we doing the right thing, what if the grass is not greener elsewhere, are we making a mistake, will we ever find someone else, someone who cares for us as much as our partner does?

How do we decide if it's the right time to call it a day?

- Over time we may gradually notice that we are becoming increasingly irritable with our partner; the things that initially attracted us to them may be starting to wear thin. Their easy-going ways may now seem boring, lazy or aimless. We've become less interested in what they say or do. Perhaps our sex lives have gradually dwindled away.

  Some of these symptoms may be due to stress. We may have a busy job, impossible deadlines, be juggling a lot of areas of our lives. Try to identify where the problems lie, take a break, start to spend more quality fun time with your partner and find time to share your mutual concerns. Relationship counselling may be a useful route to follow at this time.

- If you're sure that your feelings towards your partner have changed it may be time to acknowledge that our paths sometimes include special people, but only for a limited period of time. Recognise that he or she will always be a part of who you are; they've helped to shape your personality, they've contributed to who you are today. Give thanks for that but also appreciate that sometimes we eventually have to separate and move on in different directions.

- Stop and consider the consequences of staying with someone out of pity, guilt or fear of causing them distress. How humiliated and disrespected would you feel if someone did that to you? Caring for someone may mean saying 'I don't love you in the way you deserve to be loved'. This can be a very painful conversation, but ultimately it may need to be done.

- If you decide to stay in your relationship will you look back in five years' time and regret not leaving sooner? Family pressures, financial concerns and emotional distress can cause a lot of pressure but staying with someone for the wrong reasons can result in slowly growing to despise them, become increasingly resentful and maybe even causing health issues.

- Communications are an important part of a good relationship. Falling out of love but remaining good friends can sometimes happen when open and honest channels of communication have been maintained throughout. Talking things through ensures that there are no surprises, both people know how each other feels and, as such, decisions can be shared, understood and agreed together. Listening is a key part of this process.

- Caring for another person means wanting what's best for each other, even if that doesn't include staying together. And equally, if we come to realise that we've fallen out of love, it's about respecting the other person enough to give them the chance to find someone who does want them, who will love them as they deserve to be loved.

Holding onto someone out of fear of making the wrong decision, or because of concerns at ending up alone and lonely is both hurtful and disrespectful. Sometimes taking a break or even ending the relationship allows both parties time to miss each other and re-evaluate what it means to them. If you're meant to be together the time apart will enable you to appreciate each other all the more, give an opportunity to clear your head and have a period of reflection, so that you can become completely sure about the importance of the relationship in both your lives.

Dealing with the Loss of a Loved One

There are certain days of the year that hold especial significance after a loved one has died. Birthdays, anniversaries and even National Bereavement Day can be times when we stop and catch our breath. For some people these dates may be a little like Thanksgiving, a day set aside to pause and remember those close relationships or members of their family who are sadly no longer with them. These are times when we can reflect on what's really important in our lives.

A significant date can be used to be nostalgic, to remember our loved ones, the special people who we spent time with and commemorate their passing. One tribute to those people no longer with us is to live our lives as well as we can. But some bereaved people struggle to move on, feeling that it is disrespectful to do so. They may feel that it's important to honour the dead person's memory by continuing to do what that person wanted.

But those people who loved and cared for us would want us to be happy and fulfilled after their death. They would want us to honour their memory by being true to ourselves and lead satisfying lives.

Let's consider what can happen when someone dies and look at the process of grieving. Let's also recognise that many other kinds of loss can equally can cause the distress of grief. The ending of a significant relationship, a missed opportunity, redundancy, loss of health or lifestyle can all cause feelings of bereavement. In these circumstances the process of healing and recovery is very similar.

Several stages make up the cycle of grief and loss. These stages may be experienced several times and in any order until the process is exhausted:

- Shock is often the first feeling experienced. This comprises of numbness, disbelief or perhaps even no feeling at all.

- Denial often follows, as 'I don't believe it, it's not true.' A refusal to accept the loss is often part of the reaction at this stage.

- Bargaining can include negotiation, as in 'if I promise to do this, will you make it right'. This stage is often directed to God, a higher power or to whoever is deemed to be responsible.

- Anger can last some time. Rage, frustration and fury is often about trying to make sense of what has happened, anger that nothing can be done to change things, whilst struggling to come to terms with it. 'Why me, after all I've done, it's not fair' are often the sentiments expressed at this stage of the process.

- Depression and grieving can become all-consuming. Crying, not knowing or caring what happens next, the future appearing pointless and bleak are often part of this phase of the cycle. It's important to be gentle with oneself at this time.

- Acceptance is the ultimate stage of the process, a feeling that the loved person lives on through oneself, any children, memories, photographs and even lifestyle. Some people are concerned that acceptance of a close death is a betrayal or negation of the dead person's life, but in many ways it is a celebration of their importance to us, as we continue living the life we started out together.

Anniversaries and specific days provide an opportunity to reflect on the significance of those special relationships, the loved people, now no longer with us. For other people it may be that they mourn and remember a pet who was especially important to them, a loved animal who was their close companion and friend. Taking time to celebrate the time we spent together, to read letters, play music or look at photographs may be a special way in which to remember them.

Family, friends, counsellors or our faith are all important ways of finding support after a loss or death. Sometimes other people are unsure as to what to say, they don't want to be hurtful, appear insensitive or say the wrong thing, so it can be important to give them some insight into what might help or provide comfort. Loss and bereavement are times of mutual learning, about ourselves, each other and about how to handle the difficult times in life.

Healing and recovery also eventually include an appreciation of how far we have come since the loss. It's important to reflect on how proud the departed would be at what we have done with our lives, how supportive they would want to be of our distress and how amused they'd be at our clumsy attempts to do their 'jobs'.

Some people find that bereavement counselling and hypnotherapy can provide important solace and comfort after a death. Understanding the various stages of grief, learning ways to cope and heal and then ultimately moving into recovery are all steps on the road to wellbeing again.

CHAPTER FOUR

Stress and Friends

The Importance of Friends

Some people number their friends in the dozens. They like to feel popular and in demand and love being welcomed and recognised everywhere they go. Other people prefer to travel light; they like to be independent and unencumbered by people and relationships. We're all different, but the optimum level is probably somewhere in-between, knowing many people with whom we're friendly with but having a small select group of true friends, the ones who form our inner core.

Apart from anything, having many friends can be difficult to sustain. Keeping those relationships nurtured can be a daunting commitment. It's time-consuming and expensive, as well as emotionally and physically draining. It can be great fun for a while, receiving lots of invitations and requests, constantly replying to texts and calls, but it's impossible to be everywhere as well as tend to our other responsibilities.

Over time we may find that we start to become more discerning. We may begin to realise that we prefer some people to others or that some activities are better suited to our tastes. We may find that we start to become more selective and take control in order to better manage our friends and our time.

Being a loner can be fine, but as a way of life it can become a rather isolating choice. Human beings tend to function better when part of a group, even if that entails being in several different groups that cover work, social and life choices. Being connected to others in both physical and emotional ways encourages good health and wellbeing. Other people can provide a wealth of support. Having friends can be the inspiration behind us making an effort.

True friends are people who care about us and our wellbeing.

- They motivate and encourage us in our plans. It can be easy for us to be complacent and stay in our comfort zone or say that we'll make an effort 'next week'. Friends are often good at giving us a nudge to get started and have a go. And they may even volunteer to join us in our endeavours.

- A good friend will listen when we need to be heard, will not pass judgement and will try to understand and empathise with how we're feeling. There will no doubt be plenty of times when they hear the same story, possibly several times over, but they'll still be there for us in a supportive way. Equally there may be times when they tell us to be quiet, stop talking about it and move on. Enough is enough! And that can be useful to hear on occasion.

- Honesty is important from a friend. Knowing that they'll be honest and say if they feel we're behaving inappropriately, are in danger of doing something they suspect is a mistake or are wearing something that looks completely wrong. We can trust their opinions because they care and are looking out for our best interests.

- Loyalty is an important commitment from a friendship. A good friend will not criticise or say hurtful things about us to others. If we do something silly or make a fool of ourselves they will stand by us and help us to pick up the pieces. They may laugh and tell us off, but they'll then support us as we recover, help put the situation into better perspective and encourage us to move on.

- Friends teach us about being selfless too. Considering someone else, occasionally doing something because it matters to them, being sensitive to their needs, concerns and how they're feeling is important. True friendship is a two-way relationship, which sometimes involves giving more than we take, but then other times taking more than we give. It adds meaningful connections to our lives.

There may be times when friends will move on and out of our lives. We may relocate to another area, change our job, completely makeover our life and as a consequence move into a different world of friends. That can be fine. Not everyone's able to retain their friends throughout their life. But some friendships will survive moving away, the demands of a career or family and the ups and downs of life. Modern technology can assist in keeping in touch more readily.

Unlike family, friends are the people we've chosen to have in our lives; we've been drawn to them for a variety of reasons. For a time we're able to share mutual interests, affection and concerns. And, as such, we're able to benefit each other's lives in many positive, constructive and fun ways.

Friends - An Important Part of our Support System

Some people refer to everyone they know as a friend, but they're probably more likely to be 'people we're friendly with' because true friends are the people with whom we have a true and caring connection.

We don't need to have known a good friend for a long time. Sometimes it's possible to form an instant empathic connection with a relatively new acquaintance, where that person becomes an important ally and close friend quite quickly. I recommend spring-cleaning our friends from time to time, as it's possible to keep unhelpful people in our lives just because they've always been there, even when they've become a negative or unfortunate influence.

Some people like to be fair weather friends. These people are great fun to be around, love to socialise and enjoy adventures, but they have their limitations. They can't cope for too long with a crisis or when advice is needed. If we're able to focus on their good points they can be a valuable distraction from problems and provide a fun outlet whenever we meet up. But they prefer life to have no complications or messiness.

Other people are good at being foul weather friends. These people are great problem solvers and are incredibly supportive throughout the difficult times. They may not be interested in a lively social life or want to party very often. They detest going out drinking and mixing with lots of other people, but they are reliable, trustworthy allies and a great support to have around.

Many people are a complex mix of both fair and foul weather friends. They are people with whom we share lots of different times and experiences. They appreciate that sometimes we are sad, mixed-up or confused, but they don't judge us harshly for that. They know that we have valid reasons for the way we feel and they're able to understand. They also appreciate that most of the time we're fun to be around and that, whenever required, we're equally supportive of them.

Having friends is also a valuable lesson in life. They teach us about sharing, being aware of someone else's point of view and having a wider perspective on many different situations. Being respectful of people and the way they live their lives is an important part of building close relationships. It's fascinating to listen and learn about others, understand and be tolerant of their different relationships, and to learn how they think and interact.

Being Friendly is a Great Way to Manage Stress

Modern life is often stressed, busy and lived at a fast pace. Sometimes there can seem to be no space in the day to pause and take time over the niceties of life, the pleasantries and interesting follow-up conversations that once were so lovely to enjoy after the essential business had been dealt with. Those might be rare moments, taken to smile, chat, and enquire after someone's health, holiday, cat or mother but they are often the moments that stay with the other person long after any business has been conducted.

Newly single people, newcomers to an area and people hoping to widen their circle of friends often start the process by making the effort to attend somewhere new for the first time. They're looking to meet interesting, like-minded people. In order to start building new relationships they have to learn the value of making pleasant small talk and being engaging and friendly towards other people.

Being friendly adds a positive dimension to situations and relationships.

- It helps ease tense situations. When the atmosphere is friendly people are able to relax and be themselves. People are less fearful, tense or defensive if they feel that people around them are friendly.

- It gets the best out of everyone. Whether playing a game or being involved in a piece of work, if the atmosphere is critical or unfriendly people become nervous and stressed, fearful of making a mistake or of doing the wrong thing. A friendly atmosphere encourages people to have a go and be less self-conscious about the outcome. Even if a mistake does occur they'll be more relaxed about admitting to it, which allows it to be rectified sooner.

- Better contacts are made for the future. Relationships develop when people enjoy each other's company and try harder to support and help each. People will often bend over backwards when they like someone. It's a pleasure to help a friendly person.

- It improves confidence. People are happier to mix with others, take more chances and be more resourceful when they feel friendly towards each other. Everyone benefits. Nervous people improve in confidence and find the courage to have a go, confident people often become more generous and supportive of others. People relax with each other and it's often surprising to see how much relationships improve as a consequence.

- People are happier to make more of an effort, work longer hours and be more flexible when the atmosphere is friendly. Appreciation, recognition and thanks are often more important than a pay rise and it's not uncommon for people to change jobs and take a pay cut in order to move to a friendlier, more appreciative working environment. A by-product of a happy atmosphere is that sick leave and clock-watching is reduced.

- Complaints are often more speedily resolved when the complainant has a friendly approach. Think of an angry, irate customer who's shouting and swearing, who's perhaps threatening in manner. That person may get attention and results, but people try harder to resolve a problem or complaint when they're approached in a civil, 'let's sort this out' manner. Better results occur after calmly explaining the problem and being friendly towards the person who's dealing with it. They're more likely to make an effort to try to resolve the matter when they're treated in a friendly, respectful way.

It seems hard to imagine the difference that being civil and polite can make, but being friendly improves every area of our life.

Top Tips for Making Friends

There are occasions when we've all been the new kid on the block where we've been keen to fit in and make some new friends. It may have been the first day in school, walking into a new job, starting out in a different neighbourhood, or we may have been newly single, coping with a brand new way of life. Sometimes others may be sharing our first day struggles too; other times it may be that we've had to deal with them on our own.

Whatever the situation let's look at some tips to engage with new people:

- Give yourself a mental advantage by keeping up-to-date with the news, with things that are happening in your area and even the popular programmes on TV, especially if you think that those topics will be of interest to the people you'll be mixing with. Being able to contribute to conversations helps you to be more relaxed and able to be yourself, rather than standing self-consciously on the side-lines.

- Ask some questions of the people you meet and be genuinely interested in their replies. Remember what you've been told, so that you can follow-up on the conversation in the future. It makes other people feel interesting, valued and helps them to remember you.

- Be friendly, but don't try too hard. Accept that there are times when others may not be interested in becoming your friend; they may have a lot on their mind, be stressed or busy and dealing with their own problems. Their reasons will have nothing to do with you, but it could make them seem aloof, stand-offish and preoccupied. Relax; don't take disinterest or rejection personally and move on.

- If it's your first day in a new work environment try to quickly learn the basics, like people's names, where the facilities are and where everything is kept. Keep a notebook and make comprehensive notes as you're told your various duties. These notes will mean that you don't have to keep asking questions and instead are able to relax, feel less stressed and confidently participate, ready to start building friendly relationships with your co-workers.

- Go regularly to places that interest you, like the gym, a social club or night school classes. By attending on a regular basis you're more likely to see the same faces and come into contact with people who are interested in the same things as you, hopefully in a relaxed, informal environment.

- Accept invitations and suggest events that you think may be of interest to those in your circle. Whether at work, with other parents at your children's school, people at your gym or your neighbours, there may well be opportunities to mix and meet socially, so opening the possibility of making friends.

- Local theatres, concerts and societies often have mailing lists that you could sign up for. Many venues have promotional events; two for the price of one, happy hours, ladies evenings or televised football. Familiarise yourself with what's available in your area and offer to organise something. That way you get to know a lot of people fairly quickly and become a pivotal part of the group.

- Suggest a coffee at yours as a reason to get together. It's an inexpensive way to share a little time with the people you meet on a regular basis and gives you the chance to share time in a relaxed informal way, establishing some friendly foundations in those relationships.

- If you feel that you have low self-esteem or underlying issues that are holding you back from trusting others or being friendly, consider having counselling or hypnotherapy. This is an effective way of recovering from past experiences, bad habits and unhelpful behaviour and can enable you to improve your confidence and self-belief.

There is a saying that if you go halfway to meet someone they will usually be prepared to meet you halfway too. Most people want to be friendly and, even if they don't become your new best friend, using these tips will help you to establish a reasonable social life with people who are good to be around.

When Young People Have to Make New Friends

There are times in life when young people have to accept that it's time to start over and make new friends. They may have moved school, have fallen out with their old friends or are simply feeling restless and dissatisfied with their existing friendships. It's time to move on, introduce new people and interests and enjoy a change.

Here are a few hints for young people at this time:

- It may be important to first look at improving your confidence and self-esteem levels. Some young people find the idea of making friends from scratch an unnerving prospect; who would want to be their friend, how do they start? First reflect on all your good qualities, the things you do well, the fact that you have people in your life who like and accept you as you are. Remind yourself of your attributes, stop the negative self-talk and allow a more positive attitude and outlook to emerge.

- Identify what interests you, the type of music you like, the things that you enjoy. There is no point in regularly agreeing to go on shopping expeditions, watch football matches or attend concerts if you're really not interested in those things. Decide what you do like, what appeals to you and then locate a club, group or society which provides regular meetings where you can mix with people who share those interests.

- Take your time with potential new relationships. If you go somewhere regularly, like the shopping mall, social club or sports track, what about those people who go at a similar time to you? Smile and say 'hello'. There's sure to be an opportunity where you can strike up a conversation, discuss what they're doing, ask if they have time for a coffee or would perhaps be interested in seeing a film sometime. At school there are opportunities to chat on a more regular basis, to discuss homework, teachers, other school friends and grow a relationship more steadily.

- Notice how other people socialise. Social skills are learned through trial and error. In nursery school new children usually stand to one side and watch how the group interacts before they decide to join in. They determine which children they like, who they'd feel most comfortable with, learn what is regarded as 'normal' behaviour and discover where they'd be accepted. As we become a little older forming new relationships is no different. Discovering what is regarded as acceptable in a group enables a newcomer to adapt and fit in more readily.

- Be flexible. Sometimes it's important to have a go and try new experiences. Saying 'yes' to opportunities is important as a way of expanding your circle of interests, but it's important not to regularly go along with things out of a desire to please others, fit in or be accepted. Doing that is a recipe for long-term frustration and unhappiness. Plus it sends out the wrong message; that you like and are interested in things that you're really not that keen on.

- Accept invitations. Whilst it's not a good idea to regularly do what you don't like to do, occasionally going somewhere new, even somewhere that may not sound too appealing can be a useful introduction to new people or interests. And you may surprise yourself at how well the opportunity turns out.

- Rejection shouldn't necessarily be taken personally. Sometimes people are busy doing other things, are not especially keen on your suggestion or are genuinely not available. Remember, there are times when you too will have to decline invitations for similar reasons. Be pragmatic, maybe ask for feedback on your suggestions and focus on developing the people and activities that appeal to you.

- Keep positive and have a second choice up your sleeve. If there are times, even on your birthday, when you've nothing arranged, use that time to do things that you like; maybe suggest things to share with family. Let your family look after you, give you treats and spoil you. Choose your favourite things to eat, spend an evening watching a film that you've long wanted to see, use the time to read a book or listen to music and enjoy having time for yourself.

Accept that not everyone in life will be a special friend. Over time we all acquire an assortment of people who are great friends, but some may be limited to specific spheres of our lives; some may be great pals at school, others may be people we spend time with in our neighbourhood, then there's our family and, as we get older, work colleagues are added to the mix.

Appreciate the different relationships and accept their varied roles in your life and even their limitations. Enjoy the different opportunities that these relationships present. By adopting a more chilled attitude you may well find it easier to make new friends, have a full social diary, gain several real friends and acquire many interesting activities along the way.

Is This Person Really a Friend?

Many of us have friends who are at times a disappointment to us. They perhaps let us down, treat us badly or do not respect us in the way that we respect them. Sometimes we can shrug it off, but other times we may decide that we have to address it, decide how we feel about the relationship and whether or not we want to keep that person in our life.

Adult relationships often require us to acknowledge that different friends fulfil us in different areas of our lives; they satisfy different interests and needs, and that is okay. We may have friends with whom we chat about serious matters, like our personal problems. Others, we may spend fun and social time together. Some people may be purely work-related friends, so with them we discuss in detail issues, projects and plans relating to work commitments. Many people will have an impact on our lives, and often they'll never meet each other because they belong to completely separate areas of our lives.

What happens if a friendship starts to falter; what do we do when a friend:

- **Treats us badly**. In any relationship we have to take some responsibility for the way we are treated. Eleanor Roosevelt said that we teach people how to treat us, but that said, it can be a shock, a source of real distress when someone who is supposed to be our friend treats us with disregard or disrespect. It's important to stand up and address the situation as soon as is reasonably possible. If our friend is going through a bad patch or is seriously stressed then there may be understandable reasons for their behaviour, but we have to be firm and establish that they must stop taking their frustrations out on us.

- **Lets us down**. Childless friends can sometimes struggle with the commitment that a parent has to their children. Working people will usually have different priorities to their non-working friends. Understanding that children have to come first, even when they're being unreasonable, or that a demanding client or boss needs to be appeased can sometimes be a pre-requisite of being a loyal, considerate friend. If, however, regular cancellations occur maybe consider including that unreliable friend in group arrangements, so that if they have to pull out at the last-minute at least the arrangements can go ahead. That way the pressure is taken off the busy friend and everyone can feel more relaxed about the relationship.

- **Lies to us**. Honesty is an important part of a friendship. If we discover a friend has been lying to us it can undermine the whole basis of the relationship and it can be difficult to trust them again. A first step can be to try to establish all the facts, ask them what has been going on, tell them what you have discovered and ask to hear their side of the story. It's important to understand the different points of view before reacting to one version of events. A story often has a completely different bias when told by two different people. And sometimes a person may lie because they don't know what else to do, for a myriad of reasons. Discussing this and saying how you feel can clear the air for both of you for future eventualities.

- **Fails to reciprocate**. Sometimes there is one person in a relationship who regularly makes lots of effort, organising trips out, making plans, motivating and organising, whilst the other blithely lets that happen without any sign of appreciation or acknowledgement. After a time it can be relevant to stop and assess what's going on. If that person is happy to give without receiving thanks, then that's fine, but sometimes boundaries need to be introduced. This may mean that various tasks are allocated within the relationship, help is asked for or being generous stops when the giver starts to feel resentful or taken for granted.

- **One-way generosity**. For example, a person may host meals and coffee mornings for friends but never get invited back. After a while it may be worthwhile to stop doing them and see if the others notice. It may be that someone else realises what's happened and decides to be proactive, or that the others in the group didn't really notice, so they stop altogether. Sometimes one person enjoys doing something and others in the group are happy to go along with it. They enjoy them, but are not prepared to go to the trouble of hosting events themselves.

Sometimes it can be useful to mentally spring clean our friends and clear out the frenemies. Otherwise we can accumulate people in our lives whom we humour, tolerate and make an effort for, but who in reality we have long since outgrown. Sometimes good manners or guilt feature and we feel honour bound to keep them in our lives. It's valid to acknowledge that they were once an important part of our lives, but we have now moved on. And just like those old names on our Christmas card list, we cross them out of our lives.

The Best Way to Support a Friend Through Their Divorce

Divorce is nowadays such a frequent occurrence that many of us find ourselves at times needing to be supportive of a friend who's struggling to come to terms with their breakup. We may even be in need of a friend's support ourselves at some point.

Everyone is different and each of us experience loss and hurt in our own way. Some people may be devastated to have lost the love of their life. Others may be relieved that their difficult, loveless ordeal is finally over. For some the breakup may mean public humiliation or financial hardship. There are many personal considerations unique to each situation.

Friendships can be severely tested when one person is dealing with the trauma of a breakup. They may become preoccupied, bitter or distraught as well as having to cope with many practical matters that take time and drain their emotional energy. Emotions often run high, tension can be a daily state and life can feel like a never-ending crisis. It can be especially tough as a friend, especially if you have been friends with both parties or appreciate the other person's point of view.

Let's look at ways you can help your friend at this time:

- **Listen**. Sometimes your friend may simply need you to listen whilst you let them have their say. They may not want advice or opinions, but simply need you to be there whilst they vent and get things off their chest. People often feel better for simply having verbalized their distress. It can provide a release.

- **Call time on the talking**. But if you feel that your friend has become obsessed or preoccupied with their ex and has no other topic of conversation, constantly repeating the same story, their old grievances over and over again, there can come a time when it's important to introduce other topics into the conversation. This does not negate or disrespect their hurt. It simply allows them and you to have a break from the constant re-infecting of those old wounds. It allows them to become more receptive to outside life.

- **Encourage them to try counselling and hypnotherapy**. If you feel that your friend has issues or bad habits that have been a factor in the divorce it can help to suggest that they address those problem areas. Seeking therapy can start them on the path to resolving those issues, improve their understanding of the situation and feel better about themselves and their prospects with any future relationships.

- **Try not to take sides**. Being supportive and empathising with your friend is important but joining in and adding to the situation benefits no one. It may simply succeed in prolonging the anger and any negative feelings.

- **Consider the children.** If your friend has custody of the children they may need some support and help with looking after them if they are unused to being with them alone. Fathers often find that having the children for set visitation periods is quite stressful at first. They want to make the times together as fun as possible but are often inexperienced at entertaining the children alone for sustained periods. They often struggle with how contrived it feels. Mothers may need additional babysitting support at times, especially if they need to start working or want to socialise occasionally.

- **Encourage good habits.** When a person is distressed they may forget to take proper care of themselves. Encourage them to shop, eat, wash and sleep well. It may be a thoughtful gesture to invite them to stay with you for a little while, if you're in a position to do so. Try to discourage excessive alcohol consumption. Alcohol is a depressant but it can be seen as an escape or a comforting habit when a person is feeling low.

- **Give support to outside interests.** Encourage healthy interests like sport, volunteer work or training courses, activities that include other people and which can offer an engaging distraction. Often divorce gives people more free time and less money, which can leave people at a loose end. Suggest positive ways for your friend to spend their free time.

Supporting a friend through their divorce can be an intensive and demanding period in everyone's lives. The phrase 'start as you mean to go on' can be useful to remember. In the initial days a person may need a lot of support, but as time goes on it can be important to find opportunities which encourage them to become more independent. Try to include other friends and interests in your lives. That way you introduce a healthier approach to life and a more positive basis for your friendship that respects and accommodates both your lifestyles.

Can My Ex and I Still Stay Friends?

After a breakup there is often much residual hurt and disappointment. People can feel a failure or they may be distraught at the hurtful things that have been said and done. Time can heal some of those feelings and eventually some people may succeed in having an amicable relationship with their ex. This is especially helpful if there are children whose welfare needs to be considered.

Let us look at ways to manage the situation from the outset.

- In the Home chapter of the book I've talked about living together after the divorce, an option that works well for some people. If that's something that you're considering, it might be useful to have a look at that section.

- No matter how fraught our relationship has become, the truth is, our ex often knows us better than anyone else. They have known us as we grew our career, tried to balance work and home, experienced the associated fears, stresses and concerns and may have supported us throughout those times. At one time we used to love each other, share special times together and feel valued and attractive in each other's company. We planned on growing old together. When an acrimonious split occurs it may be impossible for the friendship to recover, but keeping a friendly interest and concern in each other's wellbeing can work for some couples.

- It may be that you get on better after the divorce. The reasons behind the day-to-day arguments and bickering have been removed. The lingering hostility and stress does not feature anymore, so you can revert to being two separate individuals again. And, indeed it's not unheard of for a couple to get back together again after a divorce. The time apart can remind them of all that was good about the relationship and they're able to reflect and remedy where they went wrong.

- Some people commit to each other when they're very young, when they don't fully appreciate what they want from a relationship or know how to treat their significant other once dating changes into a full-time, co-habiting partnership. Then there are those who may despair when their roles change significantly after marriage and they became a stay-at-home mother or major breadwinner father.

  When they sever their relationship and spend time apart it may be that both people can reflect on their respective issues in a far calmer way. They can consider what went wrong, why they reacted the way they did and whether or not they communicated well and shared their thoughts and feelings with one another. Taking responsibility for their own behaviour can enable a couple to start talking properly at long last.

- Relationship counselling can be a useful step in helping a warring couple understand each other better, whatever the eventual outcome is after their sessions. Some couples may choose to reconcile, but others may feel that too much damage has occurred and they need to split. Often relationship counselling can help to ease the process by enabling frank, open and honest discussions, so that important insights and understanding of each other's feelings are reached.

If one person feels that the other is being unreasonable or over-reacting about a situation they can talk it through in a neutral setting, with time dedicated solely for that purpose, with no distractions. Relationship counselling can help to understand and address the reasons for any blurred lines in communications.

It may be that one person in the relationship has previously experienced harsh treatment, comes from a dysfunctional background, or has in the past fallen victim to emotional hurt, bullying or betrayal. As a consequence they may be especially sensitive to rejection or feeling disrespected. Therapy can help to improve their self-esteem, confidence and self-awareness, and enable them to cope better with the eventual outcome of the relationship. This can support a better understanding of each other after the divorce.

CHAPTER FIVE

Stress and Family

The Importance of Family

Throughout life we gradually learn, develop and grow, becoming more independent as we move through childhood, into the teenage years and then adulthood. As time progresses our family's role will change too and those people, once vital to our very survival, may seem to matter less and less. It's a natural part of the process of growing up and laying claim to our own identity.

Other external relationships may seem to be more relevant, supportive and exciting. We want to be with the people who 'get us'. It matters that we're popular, fit in, are seen to be up-to-date, well-connected and living a full and active life. Family may at times drop off our radar as the effort to consider our other relationships becomes too time-consuming.

But our own family, our parents and siblings, remain a part of us, no matter what.

- **They love us anyway.** Often parents despair at the behaviour of their children, how rude and unappreciative they are or how they consider nothing but their own comfort and interests. As time passes there may be even be problems that are more serious;

disappointments, lies, betrayal, even crime. Sometimes a family member may behave in an unacceptable way, and we may be quick to react and criticize them for it. But, woe betide, if anyone else dares to join in and speak harshly or negatively about them; family loyalty will surface we will typically become defensive and protective.

The truth is, sometimes we may not like members of our family but we do have a special connection with them. They're blood. Detaching and distancing ourselves from our blood connection can seem necessary at times, but when they're in trouble and need us there's usually no question of our support. At those times we will stand together and show our support, knowing that we can rely on them to do the same for us.

- **Family keep us grounded**. We cannot become a diva or a superstar when someone has seen us suffering from a tummy bug, stranded up a tree or covered in toffee and mud. Family are good at saying it like it is; they cannot help themselves. So the comment, look or reminder that stops us from going over the top is often a valuable nudge or reminder for us to stay real.

- **They give us honest feedback**. Family will usually give us their genuine opinions about a decision or choice that we're looking to make. However, we need to consider that there may be times when their own personal agenda is influencing them too. They may want to deter us from moving away, or they may be envious when they say that a new opportunity or relationship is not right for us. But family will usually say what they think in a way that others may not. That kind of honesty can be refreshing, especially if we're usually surrounded by non-committal people in other areas of our lives.

- **They remind us of our priorities**. When we're on an exciting career path it can be all too easy to be swept along with the appointments, meetings and lifestyle, becoming immersed in the demands of a busy schedule, but then forgetting that we have other priorities too. Family members are in a position where they can remind us of the people and things that truly matter, of what is important, the reasons why we work so hard. They can point out that we're spending too much time at work, they may notice that our children need more attention, that our partner's not coping as well as we'd thought.

- Also taking time for the important family events, new children being born, family weddings, anniversaries and even funerals can all serve to remind us of the importance of our family, of what really matters. These times can bring us closer together.

- **Communications** between family members can become complex as new partners, responsibilities and different priorities are added to the mix. Keeping a balance and a sense of perspective in family relationships is important. Some family members may feel threatened when new relationships are introduced. They may worry as to its impact on the family hierarchy and previous closeness. Jealousy and power struggles can sometimes threaten to erupt, but a sense of humour, honesty and fairness can help the situation improve. Trying to see things from everyone's different perspective can be useful.

And as each generation decides to settle down with their partners, starts to raise their own family, so the cycle repeats again. Settling down and supporting a family is often the main reason for committing to a career, for working hard and focussing on success. Each of us wants to provide a good quality of life, security and status for our family, but that pressure to provide can result in us spending increasing amounts of time away from our family. Keeping a healthy balance and not losing sight of the important priorities is also important.

Some of the stress to do well, earn money and be successful can be alleviated by reminding ourselves that children will often value a family game of football, an afternoon fishing or time spent doing crafts far more than expensive gifts which are played with alone in their room. Memories of times together are an important part of family life. Children also love to hear stories of their family heritage, about what their parents did when they were young.

Keeping in touch with our family and our roots is important, but so too is integrating the lessons we've learned over time, our family values and traditions, into our adult life. As we raise our own family we can continue the story in a way that's appropriate for where we are today.

The Importance of Father's Day

Father's Day is the time when we typically give cards, whiskey, cigars to our fathers in recognition of their valuable role in our lives. But these days many homes are single-parent families with an absentee father maybe seen only occasionally. Step-fathers, grandfathers, uncles, neighbours, teachers can all occupy the position of significant male role model and may actually be more supportive and reliable that our real father.

Their father is often a child's first significant male role model. If he falls short, is a disappointment, the child may learn to become defensive or shut off emotionally in a bid to avoid further hurt and let down and become determined to show they don't care. Or, conversely, the child may react against their treatment and become rebellious and defiant as they continue to demand attention, any attention being deemed better than none.

Let's reflect on the qualities we may feel are important in a father:

- **Physical strength** is a quality many children value in their father. Children feel proud when their father is strong and physically fit. They feel protected against whatever danger there may be in the world. Knowing that he's strong provides reassurance and a sense of security.

- **Moral strength** is important. Children like to see their father do 'the right thing', have principles and be fair. Admiring and respecting their father for his integrity, honesty and guidance reinforces their valuing of those qualities for their own future dealings with others.

- It's important to see a man, their father**, in touch with his feelings**, comfortable at expressing himself appropriately, prepared to hug, show love and affection. It's also a crucial life lesson to watch and see how he communicates, to witness the positive ways he discusses, compromises and resolves problems satisfactorily.

- **Family values**. A good father prioritizes spending time with his family. Children are especially sensitive to rejection, picking up information non-verbally through body language, behaviour and mixed messages. They register how he treats their mother as well as other family members. Good family values are learned from positive experiences.

- **Respect for others** is demonstrated in non-domestic situations. How father behaves towards other road users, staff in restaurants and shops, how he talks about and to other people. Good manners and consideration are important in building positive, successful relationships.

- **A good work ethic** is learned from a responsible father. A sense of fair play and integrity, doing a good job and gaining satisfaction from work all engender a solid foundation for life. Being responsible with money, treating property with care, not taking good fortune for granted, whilst having fun doing a good job well are traits one can hope to witness and learn from a father.

Father's Day is also an opportunity to reflect on the things we're sure we'd like to do differently. Looking to improve and do a better job whilst being determined not to repeat the mistakes that were made with us are all part of growing up and aiming to be the best we can be when we come to parent our own children.

Who are our Effective Father Figures?

The birth of his children often coincides with the time a man is working hard to establish his business, improve his career and achieve good levels of financial success and security. He's motivated to support his growing family and their escalating demands. A father often feels that he has the ultimate responsibility for earning money to finance his family; pay for holidays, school fees and a satisfactory lifestyle. It can be stressful for him to balance all the different responsibilities as well as be a good father and male role model to his children.

The demands of business can result in their father appearing to be a rather transitory or even absent figure, especially to a young child, who may be in bed when father arrives home on week nights. Some men are required to work away or be available to entertain clients, especially in the early days of their career. So evenings and weekends can be difficult times for a father as he struggles to fit in work, family and some 'me' time in which to release stress and recharge his batteries.

Step fathers are becoming an important presence in many children's lives. The dynamics of a new man on the scene can be hard to manage initially. There are several areas that often need to be negotiated with sensitivity in order to ensure that a good male role model or father figure features in the children's lives.

Acceptable behaviour and discipline can be one area that a mother and step father may need to discuss and reach agreement with. Also domestic arrangements can require sensitivity and tact, depending on the relationship with the birth father. Access visits for children can be difficult to agree in some family breakups, so legal intervention or using a genial third party, like a grandparent or family friend can be helpful. And, post-divorce it's important to safeguard the children as they can suffer from the stress of feeling that they are in the middle of parental disputes and are perhaps being used as a spy, sounding board or weapon.

Fathers are increasingly aware of the importance of being a nurturing presence in their children's lives. The ominous days of 'wait till your father comes home' for misbehaving youngsters are largely gone as more men want to be a loving, supportive presence for their children.

An increasing number of men are choosing to work fewer hours to ensure that they're home in order to see their children growing up. They want to be a part of bath time, weekends and the important events that matter to their children. There is an appreciation that children grow up quickly and those special moments cannot be revisited afterwards. Priorities may mean less money in the bank account, but some experiences matter more.

Significant male role models can come in many different guises. There are often immediate family, like birth father, step father, grandparents, uncles, and then there are the people in close proximity like neighbours and family friends. Often school teachers, coaches and tutors can have a major impact on an impressionable youngster. Then there are the media figures, celebrities, film stars and sports people who portray certain characteristics that growing youngsters may wish to emulate.

Mentoring has become an important part of young people's development programmes. Some schools have introduced mentoring programmes for those young people who have been deemed to be in need of effective male role models. In some instances sports stars or business people volunteer to give their time once or twice a month to provide advice, support and contact especially to vulnerable youngsters in need of extra support. It's regarded as a powerful way of leading by example because these mentors often have their own inspirational stories to share.

The Important Role of a Mother

A mother is usually regarded as being the heart of her home. Her primary role is initially seen as nest-building for both herself and her husband, from where they then commit to starting a family. Then her mothering instincts hopefully start to provide a safe and secure environment in which her children grow and flourish, are able to develop their personalities and talents and gain the skills to eventually move into the world as rounded human beings in their own right. Confidence and self-esteem are the two fundamental characteristics that children ideally develop from their childhood and their home environment.

In tarot cards the major card that represents the mother archetype can present in either of two diametrically opposed ways. The positive aspects can be interpreted as nurturing, caring, home building, creative, loving, and supportive. The negative aspects are often read as needy, possessive, jealous and demanding. These conflicting characteristics can be seen in many matriarchal figures, and may at different times be witnessed in one's own mother.

Problems can occur when a mother has her own issues, maybe from her personal experiences as a child. Some mothers can appear to be jealous of their own children, of their future potential, the opportunities that they are likely to have that perhaps she was denied. In other scenarios a woman may have struggled to conceive or maintain her pregnancy and when her baby is finally born she becomes an ultra-protective mother. Sometimes when a second child is born, especially if it's a long awaited boy or girl, the new born child may become the adored and doted on whilst the first born feels side-lined or unwanted from then on.

A child's world is created and affected by everything and everyone it comes into contact with. 'Normal' is a very subjective experience and each child has its own daily influences, its routine and different experiences, the sounds and events it witnesses. Saint Francis of Assisi reportedly said 'give me a child before the age of seven and he's mine for life'. Early life experiences are the basis upon which future attitudes, outlooks, opinions and habit patterns are built. They form the baseline for our boundaries, expectations, tolerance levels and fundamental core values.

Her relationships with others are an important element of what a child learns from its mother. A child witnesses how its mother treats the different people she comes into contact with, her partner, other children, her parents, friends, neighbours, even the tradespeople she deals with. Because mother is often a child's first teacher the child will absorb its mother's behaviour, her attitudes, how she deals with different situations. These lessons set in place a child's core values.

A child also witnesses how other people treat its mother, and how she reacts and responds to that treatment. Does she tolerate bad manners, is she confident and comfortable with the people she meets in various settings, how does she cope with stressful situations? All these experiences are witnessed by the child and affect its own way of handling relationships.

Good mothering gives a child the confidence to be itself, to feel accepted, loved and secure. In an ideal scenario the child will be comfortable with itself and with others, feel sure about expressing itself. But it will also have learned to be able to speak up, communicate its feelings and be respectful of other people's points of view. It will have learned to deal appropriately with criticism and disagreement and have become a balanced human being with an innate sense of self.

Bad mothering can leave an array of scars and residual damage; confusion, lack of confidence and fear of rejection. If a person has lived in an environment where they felt unloved or unlovable, second class or inferior, then those feelings can be etched very deeply. Gradually learning to trust people, form relationships and feel worthy of being treated well can start to emerge when confidence and self-esteem improve. Counselling can be valuable in helping people with inappropriate or unwanted reactions and patterns to deal with their issues and start to appreciate how and when they originated. They can begin to deal with their past experiences and allow themselves to heal well.

How to Deal with a Difficult Relationship with a Parent

Sometimes our relationship with our parents can become strained. There may be underlying tensions; we may feel that a brother or sister is the favoured sibling, or there may be specific reasons, perhaps an argument or perceived wrongdoing, which has resulted in the subsequent estrangement.

It can be difficult to reconcile ourselves to the fact that our parents are human, and are just like everyone else, as equally capable of anger, jealousy, unreasonable behaviour and resentment. But finding ways to accept and come to terms with perceived harsh or difficult treatment from a mother or father can be very difficult to deal with.

Let's look at some ways to deal with difficulties in those relationships:

- A letter can be a useful way of trying to resolve a conflict situation. It allows the writer as much time as they need to consider all the points they want to cover in detail. It can be written and rewritten as many times as is necessary, until the writer is satisfied with the content. Then the recipient can keep it to read at their leisure, mull over the salient points, take their time to think about their response, consider their options. There's no need for an instant answer with a letter.

- Even writing a letter and choosing not to send it can be cathartic. Unresolved feelings and emotions, anger and despair can be put down on paper, explained and addressed. Sometimes the process of writing a letter can be enough, but some people like to symbolically burn it afterwards, throw it out to sea in a bottle or bury it somewhere of especial significance. The ritual can be a way of finally ridding themselves of their negative feelings, the guilt, disappointment or distress.

- A person acting as a mediator can sometimes help people find a compromise in difficult relationships. It's important to find someone who's mutually acceptable and who's regarded as fair and balanced; someone who's not personally invested in the outcome of the deliberations. One parent may feel under pressure if the other parent or grandparent is involved in trying to resolve matters. Sometimes a family friend or business colleague, or perhaps a close neighbour may be seen as a reasonable compromise. The role of mediator is to keep the discussions on a positive track, to try to maintain honest and respectful communications and to move the relationship forward.

- A neutral place, perhaps somewhere public, may be a good choice for the first face to face discussion, especially if it's just the two of you meeting for the first time since the relationship collapsed. Meeting in a public place makes the situation less intense as there are often external distractions as well as the requirement to keep emotions in check and maintain good manners and civility.

- Might there be some merit in contriving to meet your estranged mother or father by 'accident'? Discovering her or his movements, maybe ending up in the same place and being able to say 'hello' or even suggest a coffee may offer a light touch in starting to break the ice.

- But ultimately we may have to accept that our mother or father has his or her own reasons for not being able to resume the relationship at this point in time. We may have to come to terms with the fact that there's nothing we can do to heal the rift for now, leaving no choice but to walk away. Maintaining contact with other family members is a good way of keeping future options open, but we may have to reconcile ourselves to the estrangement, for the time being at least.

Counselling and hypnotherapy can play a valuable role in helping us understand and deal with our own emotions and sense of loss at this time; the grief, distress and perhaps guilt at what has happened. It can help us to view the situation from a better, more helpful perspective and move forward in a balanced way, learning to take care of ourselves in the process.

From Mother to Mother-in-Law

As her offspring start to become young adults, busily engaged in developing their own relationships, gradually becoming more independent, a mother may look forward to the time when her children are off her hands, settled in their own lives. She may hope to eventually become a grandmother, with all the satisfaction and pleasure that comes from that role. The reality is often a little less straightforward than that. The progression from mother to mother-in-law can be a diplomatic tightrope, especially at first.

What is it about becoming a mother-in-law?

Even the nicest of mothers can have their well-intentioned actions misinterpreted as interfering or over-possessive when they become a mother-in-law. Their new son or daughter-in-law may feel threatened by the dynamics of their family-in-law, especially if their own experiences of family life were quite different. Jealousy may be a factor as the desire to be the most important person in their partner's life becomes stronger. Changing status from boyfriend or girlfriend to husband or wife can cause tensions to occur and perhaps even a power struggle to arise.

Some families have grown up sharing everything, all the details of their lives, on a regular basis. Becoming a mother-in-law may mean that such intimacy stops as the new living arrangements start to take priority. Even a couple who have lived together pre-marriage can experience little changes afterwards. Loyalties change and a spouse expects to have more say, more influence and first claim on their partner's time and attention than their other relatives.

A new son or daughter-in-law is often keen to be accepted, wants to be welcomed as a new addition to the family. But upgrading their role to spouse can cause a visible shift in the family dynamics. In many families there is a significant difference between the role of boyfriend or girlfriend and partner. Everyone is all too aware of the subtle distinction and this can be difficult for a mother to accept, especially if she was very close to her child or regularly involved in the details of the couple's life before they married. Taking a step back can be hard to implement.

Some couples start their married life by living together under the same roof with one of their families. This may be a practical or economic necessity but can be problematical, as the logistics of accommodating each other's cooking needs, establishing separate routines and timetables may be complicated.

A mother may be tempted to ease their burden by offering to cook, do the laundry, clean, and indeed she may be happy to help if she has the time and has always done those chores. A new daughter-in-law may perceive such an offer as subtle criticism; that she is not good enough or is viewed as having an inferior way of doing things. She may feel that she wants her and her husband to do their chores together.

Making their own mistakes and finding their own way of doing things can be an important part of a couple starting this new phase of their lives. It may take a little time and include a few disasters, but that is often a part of their journey. A mother-in-law may know that she can help but that help has to be offered tactfully and with sensitivity. That offer of support or help can sometimes be enough to convey understanding, support and empathy.

Occasionally taking her new daughter-in-law out for lunch or a coffee can be a relaxed way of demonstrating friendship and support. A good relationship can develop as the two of them start to communicate as individuals, taking time to bond away from home in an informal, neutral setting.

Arguments between the couple can be a difficult area, as a mother often wants to intervene and protect her child from hurt and distress. When one person confides in their family it can be hard not to get involved, take sides, give advice or agree with whatever negative things have been said or done. The problem is that things said cannot be unsaid and can remain in people's minds at future gatherings.

Taking sides can create tension between members in a family, cause ongoing embarrassment and make any attempts at reconciliation tougher. Relationship counselling can be a better option for a couple working through difficulties in their marriage as it provides a neutral environment for them to address their issues and work out the best way forward.

Start as you mean to go on is a good rule of thumb. Starting out as a newly married couple can bring its own honeymoon period, but it's important to quickly establish good habits that suit both sides long-term. Being tolerant and honest, whilst maintaining a sense of humour and perspective can set in place good routines and 'rules' over areas like visiting each other's in-laws, mutual respect, privacy and those other niggles that can eventually start to erode good will and cause major tensions and disharmony within families.

Should I Stay at Home or be a Working Mother?

Some women can feel that they have no real choice about working after they have had children. They may need to work to support their family and lifestyle, they may want to maintain their career, or it may not occur to them that they are in a position where they can choose to stop working and stay at home. Often though, working and non-working mothers regard each other with no small measure of envy.

Many working mothers look with longing at the life of the stay-at-home mum. They may see how easy her life appears to be. While they spend their time racing around trying to be a full-time career woman and mother, shopping, cooking meals, cleaning the house, trying to make parents' evenings on time, as well as satisfy the requirements of a demanding job, they see the non-working mother as a lady who lunches, has her nails done, goes for coffee mornings, has all the time in the world.

Interestingly the stay-at-home mothers may have a more leisurely, less frenetic lifestyle but they often look at the working mothers with envy.

Here are some interesting statistics:

Results from Pew Research pooled data covering 2003-2012 reported on the differences between the way that stay-at-home and working mothers spent their time. It showed that stay-at-home mothers spent more time on childcare (18 hours per week compared to 11 hours for working mothers), more time on housework (23 hours compared to 14 hours for working mothers), but that they also had more time to spend on leisure (31 hours per week compared to 22 hours for working mothers) and for sleep, including naps (63 hours per week compared to 58 hours for working mothers).

Let's consider some of the stresses affecting the working mother:

- Working mothers achieve more with their time. They are often under pressure to fit so much into each day that they need to stay focused on making every minute count. There's a saying that if you want something doing ask a busy person, and that is often the case. A busy person commits to doing something important straight away, feels they have to or it may not get done. Someone with lots of time on their hands may delay and defer doing something until they get around to it.

- Working women often have a wider circle of friends and acquaintances. Stay-at-home mothers often mix and meet with their own regular group of friends. A working mother will often have several groups of people whom she gets to know quite well. It makes for an interesting and varied mix of contacts and friends, though it can be quite stressful to nurture the relationships and maintain ongoing contact with them all.

- Independence is often valued by the working mother. Earning her own money, with which to help support the family and some for her to spend as she pleases, can help her feel more self-sufficient and confident. The stay-at-home mother may receive an allowance or even full access to the family's income, yet she may still feel envious of women who are independent and earning money of their own.

- Career advancement is able to be maintained by remaining in a work situation. When a woman decides to stay at home full-time she loses her seniority, experience and contact with her professional world. Some ladies may continue to renew the memberships of their professional bodies but they are often out of the work environment, sometimes for several years. Keeping in touch with her profession or career, even on a part-time basis, can keep those skills and contacts up-to-date.

- Yet many working mothers often experience guilt and frustration at their situation; they may feel under pressure to justify their decision to work, yet struggle to feel satisfaction at what they actually achieve. They're often unable to commit 100% to work; what if the children are unwell, the school is unexpectedly closed for a day or they need to leave for a parent's evening, school play or sports day? Being pulled in two directions is often their lot; wanting to advance in their career whilst spending enough quality time with their children.

- We can forget to appreciate what we have when we live with it on a daily basis. Working mothers are often all too aware of the importance of enjoying time on a daily basis with their family, of the benefits of having free time to enjoy a manicure or a lunch with friends. Sometimes the stay-at-home mother can take these things for granted and accept them as an automatic part of her daily life.

All situations come with pluses and minuses. We can look at a person in the opposite situation to ourselves and imagine how much better our life would be if we were in their shoes. Finding balance and satisfaction in our role is the key to attaining a positive quality of life, to appreciating what we have and living each day as fully as possible.

My Children are My World

For many people having a family is regarded as their single greatest achievement. We often hear of celebrities saying that the births of their children were the best moments of their lives, better than scoring an all important goal, receiving a major award or appearing on the front cover of an internationally acclaimed magazine.

Yet the feeling of total unconditional love is often accompanied by sheer terror, apprehension and overwhelming responsibility and a sense that life will never be the same again. There is awe at the task that lies ahead, at the prospect of raising healthy, happy, well-balanced children, concern at doing the best job possible, a determination not to repeat mistakes that were made with them and the desire to give them the best possible start in life.

In some instances there can a temptation for parents to live vicariously through their children, to re-live their youth by proxy, to pursue their own unfulfilled hopes, dreams and ambitions in ways that weren't available to them, a determination to make their children their entire world.

But who's to decide what matters most in life? Whilst one parent may feel that academic excellence is most important another may regard sporting achievements as the main focus in life. If a child is not interested or motivated in these areas it can be difficult for them to feel the same level of enthusiasm and commitment or, more importantly, become clear about their own individual identity and purpose in life.

Feeling pressure to please their parents by doing something they don't want or enjoy can create a crisis in a child, can cause them to doubt the value of their wishes, negate their self-belief and cause them to feel that they don't fit in, are stubborn and difficult or are in the wrong. Encouraging children to do their best whilst following their own path in life provides the opportunity for both parents and children to nurture and cultivate their individual interests, focus on their future goals in life and work on their independence, confidence and self-belief.

As children grow, the dynamics of the parent/child relationship changes and parents stop being the world to their children. From being nurse, teacher, supporter, carer some parents then want to become best friends with their child, share details of each other's lives, have their child tell them 'everything'. Being curious to know 'everything' can demonstrate genuine interest and support, but growing children need to have private corners in their lives, things they don't necessarily share with anyone or everyone, especially their parents.

Teenagers and young adults start to form relationships with other people where they gain the confidence to discuss details of their lives, compare experiences, empathise about their growing pains. Some topics may be deemed unsuitable for parents' ears and this time is important in learning how to communicate effectively with other people outside the family group.

Parents who insist on knowing every detail, every who, why, what of their children's lives can be regarded as invasive, intrusive and voyeuristic. A sensitive child may become inhibited, secretive or feel guilt, apprehension and stress about doing things with friends for fear of the parental inquisition afterwards.

A close parental relationship should be supportive, allow the child to volunteer their news and concerns rather than feel obligated to share; it should encourage them to feel confident in asking for help or advice if and when they need it.

Many parents are keen to offer financial support to their older children and help them with their start into adult life. Some may support their first step onto the property ladder, so enabling them to buy their first home and make a new life for themselves. This may then be followed with advice, help with decisions about decor, furniture, improvements, which may all feel like loving input, but does it help children discover their own taste, sample their own ideas, find their feet and feel proud of each achievement and decision? They may avoid making mistakes, gratefully accept the financial input but when does enough become too much?

What about their front door key? Whilst it may be convenient to have a key for occasional deliveries, visits from workmen and emergencies some parents find themselves calling regularly, 'just' to help with the tidying up, doing a little cleaning, ironing a few clothes, checking the post. It's important to examine the motives behind these actions and ask what's really going on. Are your children too much your world; is it time to commit to investing in new friends and other interests?

Respecting one's children as they become confident adults can be a difficult transition for a parent. From being the most important person in a child's world it can be hard to watch a young adult gradually move away from his/her parents, make mistakes, investigate their own opinions and tastes and make their own decisions, choices and occasional mistakes.

And yet it can be lovely for parents to enjoy a different, adult relationship with their children as they become free to reclaim their own lives, interests and time. Why not appreciate the invitation to visit the children for dinner, enjoy being a guest in their home and celebrate becoming grandparents. Adapting any relationship takes time, sensitivity and understanding from both sides but can offer the beginning of an exciting new phase in everyone's life.

When Someone Else has to Look After Our Children

Letting go of being the total provider and carer for all our children's needs can be a major step in any parent's life. It can bring many issues to the surface. There is the huge challenge of finding someone who we feel is capable of doing the job to our standards. Then there are the mixed emotions of handing over our precious charges to some else's care. Often there are house rules that we want respecting. A plethora of issues can arise when we someone else has to look after our children.

It's not an uncommon predicament to require help with looking after the children. A single parent may need to earn a wage or both parents are committed to their careers. Childcare may be required to enable both parents to finance their lifestyle. Some people may be able to rely on family or friends whilst others may need to hire someone else to do the job.

The problem with someone looking after our children is that whilst they come highly recommended, qualified or well-intentioned, they often have different standards or attitudes to childcare than we do. One example may be that a kind family member is lovely but is inclined to dispense regular sugary treats. Consequently our child/children come home hyper-active and difficult to settle in the evenings. If we have to rely on someone to help and can't afford to upset them we may need to deal sensitively with any issues.

Let's look at potential problems when we're in need of some help with childcare:

- It's important to accept that when we find someone our children are happy and content with, who is convenient, trustworthy and affordable we don't want to risk alienating them. Good childcare is difficult to find, but we also have to be aware of the children's best interests too.

- Guilt can be a factor when we have to rely on someone else to look after our children. We may feel guilty that we're being a bad parent, are pursuing our own selfish needs, that we're neglecting our children or are missing out on their development. But a parent who is fulfilled and positive is more likely to do a good job and appreciate their children than someone who feels resentful and trapped at home. Also many families need the income to survive and support their lifestyle.

- Could jealousy be a factor? Sometimes it can be hard to admit that we feel hurt, aggrieved and jealous at missing out on our children growing up, at witnessing significant moments in their all too short childhoods. We may be jealous of the relationship our children have with their minder. However, if they're happy, content and settled we should be happy too. We can go about our daily business, safe in the knowledge that our children are safe and secure, being looked after by someone they feel comfortable with.

- How receptive would your children's carer be to your explaining your concerns? If their diet is an issue could you tackle the subject by saying that you've seen a documentary or read an interesting article on the subject, for example, on the effect of sugar on children's behaviour? This way you're introducing your concerns in a subtle, information sharing way.

- Your childminder may have different views on raising children to you. She may think that being easy-going, with little discipline and dispensing regular treats is demonstrating love and providing them with a happy childhood. She may feel that her approach is harmless; it's how she raised her own children.

  You may need to be firm and explain your rules, that they need a nap in the afternoon, that you want them to spend time being creative or reading, that you ration your children to one treat a day. Be firm and stress that you need her to respect your decision. Explain that you have genuine concerns about their behaviour and that you are telling grandparents, friends and school about your expectations.

- Pack your children certain things that you want them to use each day; crayons, reading books, a lunch box and tell her that this is their preferred activity whilst they are with her. You could say that your intention is to minimise her work load, to avoid being a burden to her, to save her the expense of catering for your children.

Unfortunately if these strategies don't result in her adhering to your wishes you may need to reconsider your childcare arrangements. Many people find that relying on family or friends for childcare can put a strain on their relationship, as so many people have strong opinions on how children should be raised. It should help reduce your stress levels if you're able to maintain a relaxed attitude, safe in the knowledge that your children are happy and settled. This is often the key to a successful outcome.

Some Pointers on Coping with IVF

Many young people assume quite naturally that their lives will go to plan and follow the direction that they have mapped out for themselves. They feel confident that they will find that special someone, settle down together, build a home and have their 2.4 children, who have already been named!

Unfortunately, children aren't conceived to order and an increasing number of couples are turning to IVF in a bid to help them realise their dream of children and a happy family unit. Many of those people are desperate, so here are some pointers on coping with IVF to support people in that position through the process.

- **Guilt** is often an important part of the initial discovery process. When a couple first try to get pregnant they may anticipate taking a month or two for it to happen. But it can take time for their minds and bodies to adjust from having spent most of their sex lives trying not to get pregnant!

  When it becomes apparent that pregnancy is not occurring automatically each person tends to speculate about who is to blame. Is it their fault, are they responsible? Trawling through their past, wondering if their childhood mumps, abortion, misspent youth, alcohol or drugs usage was to blame can all add to the stress and make the situation more difficult to cope with.

  Therapy can be one way to deal with distress about the past and help put it into context. Any past experiences have contributed to you being the person you are today, the person your partner fell in love with. We can't change the past but we heal and let go of it in order to move on with our lives.

- **Pain** and discomfort can be a significant part of the IVF process. Tests, injections, medication, endless examinations and procedures often involve physical side effects and sometimes pain. Feeling unwell, having erratic mood swings, being strict about timed treatments can be wearing mentally, emotionally and physically. Helpful support can include pain management techniques for coping with the process.

Self-hypnosis can help. There are several techniques which enable a relaxed mental state to be entered into, whilst still being able to hear any relevant instructions. Self-hypnosis can allow a little detachment from what's going on, whilst allowing the mind and body to de-stress.

- **Patience and optimism** are an important element of the IVF process. Once the eggs have been implanted the time spent waiting to hear the outcome can seem like a lifetime. Each stage of the IVF cycle has its own timetable; being patient and keeping a positive mind-set can be especially wearing. Try to recall those other experiences of going through a process and having to wait, hoping for a good result. Studying for an exam, then awaiting the results, or attending a job interview followed by the delay before you hear the outcome can be very stressful. Hold onto the knowledge that you've done your best and it's in someone else's hands now!

- **Responsibility or blame** is another area to consider. After the tests and treatments have been undertaken one person may be deemed responsible if the IVF cycle doesn't work. How will the relationship fare if one is blamed for their childless state. Guilt, anger, shame or distress may all emerge at this time. Again hypnotherapy and relationship counselling can play an important part in supporting a couple through this difficult time of acceptance and readjustment, support them through communicating and coming to terms with their situation.

It may be that they both feel differently about the outcome of the treatment. One person may feel resentful or desperate at not being able to have children, whilst the other may feel responsible and frustrated, unable to do anything about it. At some point there may be an opening to discuss other options that may be available.

Are there other acceptable ways to bring a child into your lives, how does the relationship move forward from this, would you rather be childless and remain with your partner or is having your own child too strong a desire? And remember, if you're unable to reconcile this problem and decide to end the relationship there is no guarantee that a child would automatically be conceived in the future.

Would You Choose Your Child's Mother or Father Online?

How does the thought of choosing your child's biological mother or father online appeal to you? Does it seem a little clinical? And yet an increasing number of people are moving towards this as an option.

Nowadays online dating is an accepted, almost commonplace way of trying to find a new partner and yet in the early days it was viewed as a desperate, dangerous and rather embarrassing way of meeting people.

Yes, occasionally there are 'horror' stories of people misrepresenting themselves, using 10 year-old photographs on their profile, sometimes duping people, but those stories tend not to deter others from using the sites to meet people. Taking sensible safety precautions is recommended but many people have made successful relationships as a consequence of meeting online.

So let's consider those people who are desperate for a baby and have so far not been successful. What options are open to them? What options for the single female who is all too aware that her biological clock is ticking and that time is running out for her unless she meets someone soon, or the infertile couple who have exhausted all their available options, or the gay couple who desperately want a child of their own?

Already some of the people in these situations have taken matters into their own hands and found solutions. They may have discussed their predicament with friends and found a volunteer who's prepared to be a sperm donor or a surrogate mother; they may have roamed bars on gone online to find someone with whom they could have unprotected sex. They will have found a way to have a child as a consequence of using their own initiative.

But this is a rather random approach and in the last few years a new online method has quietly emerged where it's possible to find a potential father or mother for your child and enter into a non-legal arrangement with him or her. Tens of thousands of people have been going onto these sites, where they're able to specify what they're looking for, just as on a dating site, and then match with someone who has similar requirements.

Some people may want to co-parent, but do so within a platonic relationship. Some people may have been busy building their businesses or careers and then realised that they are fast approaching middle-age, are not in a committed relationship or in any relationship, and want to remedy their childless state.

Then there are men who are happy to be sperm donors, content to know that they have helped others and fathered children; research has shown that middle-aged sperm donors are just as fertile as those in their 20s. Some women may be happy to be egg donors or surrogate mothers, knowing that they are helping people less fortunate than themselves, that they're providing a generous service.

The aim of these sites is to allow interested parties to discuss their requirements in a confidential way and then, if they're in agreement, to be able to reach a mutually satisfactory way to proceed. No binding legal agreements feature in these relationships.

Some people may find the notion of online co-parenting distasteful, but the makeup of many families has radically altered during this century.

We may aspire to traditional family values but in many homes they are a long-forgotten memory. Let's be thankful for a child who is raised in a home where it is loved, wanted and cared for.

Guilt and the Divorced Parent

But not all relationships survive, not all parents are able to stay together, and there follows the trauma and distress of the breakup, with its subsequent impact on the children and the family. If not handled well some children can feel that they too are being divorced from their estranged parent.

Often children will live full-time with one parent and have pre-arranged access to the other. It may be that they live with one parent throughout the week and see the other parent for one or two evenings and perhaps alternate weekends and holidays. Both parents can feel guilt at the disruption to their children's lives.

Trying to respect what's best for the children and establish some basic ground rules can help both parents manage a difficult situation in the best possible way.

Let's look at some of the areas that can cause guilt:

- **Consistency in rules and discipline** can be hard to maintain when the children are coping with two separate households. The main parent often has the day-to-day routine of school, homework and after school activities to manage and consider. The absent parent often wants to make up for lost time and spend enjoyable, fun time with the children. He/she may be more lenient and regard seeing them as time for adventures and treats. It can be very disruptive when there is a clear distinction between how they are treated in both homes. Children are very quick to learn how to work the system and playing one parent against the other is an effective way to fuel guilt.

- **Money** is often a major area of readjustment after a divorce. One parent may have to manage a much tighter budget whilst the other may maintain a good disposable income. The main parent often has to spend their money sensibly on the unseen things, like food, school uniforms, gas and electricity. They can feel guilty at not being able to buy expensive trainers and gadgets for their children. The other parent often becomes the one who buys them expensive gifts and treats as compensation for not being with them as much. Both parents can feel guilty in their own ways. Money can become a means of either compounding or assuaging that guilt.

- **Food and a healthy diet** are important in supporting the wellbeing of growing children. Divorce can mean that children eat regular, healthy meals when they are with the main parent. When they visit their other parent it's not uncommon for them to eat rather differently. They may be given take-aways, burgers, fizzy drinks, snacks and then return to their main home over-excited and unwilling to settle down. Very few children will choose to eat vegetables, fruit and control their intake of sugar. They need an adult to oversee that for them. Parents have to be prepared to behave like parents and insist that their children eat and drink in a healthy way, with only the occasional treat.

- **Entertainment**. Age appropriate entertainment is important for children. This can be difficult to manage if children vary significantly in age. I have worked with parents who have been horrified when their children have returned from access visits to their other parent. They have discovered that their young children have been allowed to watch violent films, pornography or made to participate in games and sports that they were too young to enjoy or understand. Tailoring entertainment so that it's fun, age appropriate and enjoyable for all is important both for the child and for the ongoing relationship they hope to build with their parents.

The initial phase after a divorce is often a stressful time for parents and children. Children need to be able to contact both parents, spend time with them and be reassured that they're both coping. They need to feel loved and secure whilst the changes are occurring around them.

Knowing that their wellbeing is important to their parents and receiving quality attention is more important than the latest gadgets, fabulous holidays or treats. Children are very astute; they will play the system and recognise a bribe when they see one. But it doesn't mean that they mistake expensive gifts for love.

Tips for Youngsters When Their Parent's Divorce

Parents splitting up can be a time of mixed emotion for young people. Leading up to the divorce there may well have been long periods of bickering and upset or equally uncomfortable times of silence and tension in the home. Living in that environment can gradually become accepted as a normal part of everyday life.

Even though it's unpleasant and perhaps even distressing it can become all too familiar and routine. When news of their impending divorce is announced it can cause conflicting emotions to surface; relief, sadness, fear at what is to come, the impact it's going to have on everyone's lives.

When parent's divorce it may result in their children feeling obligated to take sides, to decide which one is the 'good' or 'bad' parent. They may feel torn, that they can only be loyal to one parent. This may mean that they have to demonstrate rejection or disapproval of the other. At times like this a few helpful suggestions can be useful.

Let's look at some tips to help you cope when your parents decide to divorce.

- An ally is important. Someone to talk to can make a real difference, whether it be a grandparent, schoolteacher, older sibling or family friend. It's helpful to find someone who is sympathetic and is ready to listen and support you in coming to terms with your new situation.

  It's not unusual at first to feel embarrassed or ashamed about the change in your circumstances, especially if it means moving home, changing school, having to explain why one parent is absent or why your financial freedom has become curtailed. Find someone who you feel is trustworthy, honest and impartial, someone who will not betray your secrets unless they become concerned as to your safety and wellbeing.

- You may feel that you're being disloyal to one parent if you're nice to the other, but this is their divorce, not yours. Your parents may feel differently about each other but that should not impact on your relationship with them. Yes, a period of readjustment is often needed but many parents want their children to maintain a positive relationship with both parents afterwards.

  Try to be supportive of both your mother and father during this difficult time, but be open about your feelings too. Refuse to be drawn into their dramas and speak up if you feel you're being told too much or are finding it all too much. Then you can all be there for each other in a positive, appropriate way, as you learn to move forward into this new life.

- Familiarity and routine is important at this time. Being clear about where you will live, the arrangements for school, times you'll see your absent parent, whether you're allowed to call him/her and at what times are all important facts that you need to know as soon as possible. Being aware of how the change will impact on your daily life is important.

- Refuse to be drawn into arguments or answer lots of questions about your parent's situation. If that happens you may find yourself feeling under pressure to take sides and express negative opinions. Try to explain that you don't know or don't want to answer these questions. It may help you to talk to a family friend or relative and explain that you feel that you're being placed in an unfair or difficult situation which you're struggling to manage comfortably. They may deal with that on your behalf.

- Avoid the temptation to make the absent parent, often the father, feel guilty or have to suffer because he left. It can be tempting to say 'Mum lets me do this' or 'Dad doesn't mind if I do that', but remember that your parents are learning the ropes in this situation too and are trying to put new arrangements together as quickly as possible. Avoid playing one parent against the other.

- Dad may have more money but is often the one who is now living away from home, having to start again in unfamiliar surroundings. Mum is often the one who's there for you every day, trying her best to manage on her own, frequently with less money and support. Often, though not always, both parents will have agreed to the divorce, but it's still tough for them both until things settle down.

- Accept that parents often feel guilty about their divorce. They may feel to blame because of something they did, how they behaved, the fact that their marriage failed, and may need time to recover from the breakup of the home and the disruption to all your lives. Appreciate that your parents may at times feel bad, be upset, even unwell, but equally allow yourself time to grieve.

Being able to discuss this new, unfamiliar situation is important. It helps to talk about your feelings, come to terms with them and learn that you do not have to be strong and hide your hurt and distress. Learn to be gentle with other members of your family and be mutually supportive throughout this period of change and transition.

Different Ways Grandparents Can Help Reduce Stress

Many families have times when they have to rely quite heavily on outside help to deal with the demands of daily life, especially if there has been a serious family setback like divorce, bereavement or redundancy. Grandparents can provide valuable help, advice and support, especially at times like this; they have so much to give.

- **Financial help**; grandparents often have better financial resources than their children. They may have paid off their mortgage, be retired and have less overheads, perhaps have sold their business or down-sized their home and are happy to be in a position where they can offer financial help; they may want to contribute to their grandchildren's upkeep, support their education or help out in other important ways. A grandparent's financial support can relieve serious stress from the family's shoulders.

- **Time** is something that many grandparents are happy to give, perhaps by being in a position where they have time to drop off or pick up children from school, baby sit, spend hours happily watching sports matches or concerts. Many grandparents are often happy to be able to undertake these duties and are sometimes pleased to do the things they were too busy to do when their own children were growing up. It's equally important though that you also include them in the fun times too, not just use their input when you're in desperate need of help and support. Encourage them to feel valued and appreciated as a special part of your lives.

- **Adult support** for young children can be especially valuable when it comes from a grandparent. By being older they have the advantage of usually being loved, respected and valued as a close family member whilst being experienced in life and parenting. Yet they are sufficiently detached from the immediate family group to be able to stand back and see arguments, disagreements and issues from both sides. A grandchild may be prepared to reveal their fears, concerns and problems to a grandparent but loathe to confide in their parent for fear of upsetting or adding to any existing stresses and worries.

- **Neutrality** can be important in certain situations. A parent may be too close to their recent divorce, too affected by their child's unruly behaviour or annoyed by perceived unreasonable requests. A grandparent may well be able to appreciate both points of view and act as a neutral arbiter, prepared to find areas of compromise and negotiation in difficult matters.

- **A link to the past** is important. Many children are interested and intrigued by 'long ago' times past when their grandparents were young. Grandparents are often happy to spend hours telling stories about their own childhood, their children's childhood, sharing photographs, memories and fascinating revelations about mummy or daddy when they were young. That link is important as it provides a child with roots and a feeling of security.

Grandparents can provide a safe pair of hands when children need them most. However, all too often one set of grandparents may be relied on more heavily than the other. This may be because they are logistically closer or are perceived as being more 'on side' and supportive. Valuing the important role that grandparents can play in your children's lives often introduces a richness that is unique to that very special relationship. Grandparents have much to give. But grandparents may have their own distress to cope with:

Grief and the Bereaved Grandparent

When a baby or young child dies the impact this has on grandparents is often overlooked in the midst of concern for the bereaved parents and siblings affected by the tragedy. Whether it be a miscarriage, failed IVF attempt, cot death or unsuccessful adoption, grandparents often feel that they are expected to be strong and supportive for the sake of their distressed family, feeling the need to suppress their own grief and loss out of concern for others.

As parents, their primary instinct is to support their child, to do their best to try to make things right, to protect them from harm. And yet, as impending grandparents, they have had time to fantasize and plan for their forthcoming grandchild, to imagine their role in the new child's life, to look forward to the start of a new generation. They will have dreamt about the lovely new addition to the family, imagined the joy it will bring to their lives, felt excitement for their son or daughter's new role as a parent as they add to their existing family.

Witnessing their son or daughter's devastation, sometimes hearing the news long distance, is very difficult. It's hard for them to know what to do, how to help their family and find the most effective ways to try to make it better. Coping and coming to terms with the situation as both a bereaved parent and grandparent takes time.

Let's look at some ways a grandparent can be supported at this time:

- Connecting and making contact with their son or daughter is an important first step when there's been a bereavement. Being together as a family, providing comfort, practical help, looking after each other's needs, helping them cope provides an important source of mutual understanding, especially in a close family relationship.

- Some grandparents may have to cope with their bereavement alone. They may be single, or their children live a distance away and cannot be readily visited. If their son has lost his child they may have the additional stress of feeling obliged to keep their distance if they feel that their daughter-in-law's parents take the lead and rally round to provide support.

- Relying on the closeness of friends, sympathetic colleagues and neighbours, local support groups and phone contact with family can be a means of finding immediate support, but it can sometimes be difficult for a grandparent to verbalise their feelings to others. They may feel it's inappropriate to demonstrate their devastation at the loss for several reasons.

- Sharing with their partner, husband or wife can be a help, as can sharing with someone close who has experienced a similar loss. Counselling and bereavement groups can help some people and are able to provide support, comfort and understanding.

- Acknowledging the loss of the child is important. Talking about it, admitting the extent of their grief, the implications of the young life that's been lost is an important part of the healing process. Accepting that time can help a person learn to cope better even though the memory of child remains can give permission and space to grieve.

- For some grandparents time can be an additional personal consideration. They may have concerns as to whether or not they are going to ever experience grandchildren. How long will it be before their son or daughter has a child; it may well be another year before they feel ready or able to try again. This question cannot be asked outright, even though it may be a burning issue which causes them to feel guilty for even thinking that way. It's impossible to ask the question without seeming cruel, insensitive or implying to criticise their 'failure' to produce a grandchild.

- Religious faith and spiritual beliefs can sometimes bring comfort, support and acceptance at distressing times. Even though it may be difficult, perhaps even impossible to comprehend the harshness of certain events in life, having faith in a bigger picture, a greater wisdom behind these experiences can sometimes provide the ability to accept and move forward with a degree of optimism and faith in a better future.

When It's Time for Your Children to Leave Home

The time when children start to leave home is often a source of major stress and readjustment for parents. They're often amazed at the extent of their emotions when the time approaches for their children to leave and go to college, university or on a gap year.

For some parents it can be a struggle to accept that their job is nearly over; they've done a good job, raised a happy, well-balanced child who is now confident enough to go off and explore the world. They know they should be pleased, but are conflicted as several factors often hijack their happiness and feelings of satisfaction.

Things you may experience when your children decide to move on and leave home:

- **Who am I now?** For many people their lives become completely submerged in raising their child or children. Family budgets often revolve around children, their education and support. Indeed many families continue to support their children long after they've left home as it's rare for them to earn enough to finance themselves. Hours are often spent ferrying children to various appointments, events and classes. Holidays may well be booked with the children's interests as the primary consideration.

However, once children reach the age to leave home it can highlight the fact that their parents have, over the years, dropped many of the hobbies, interests and connections they enjoyed before their children were born. It's important to start preparing for this new phase in life by identifying which interests may be fun or satisfying to introduce in anticipation of this time.

- **How do I feel about my partner?** The demands of raising a family can mean that a couple begin to feel like ships that pass in the night, often crashing into bed exhausted after work, once the demands of the day have finally been dealt with. Communication between parents can end up becoming perfunctory updates, shopping lists or instructions as the relationship slowly loses its passion and becomes more like a house share between amicable friends.

Whilst this is understandable it is also important to schedule time to nurture and maintain your relationship. In the beginning you considered your partner to be your friend, lover, ally, supporter and lifetime companion. You were two young people, in love, with shared goals and dreams of building a home and having a family and a life together. Continue to look after your relationship and aim to schedule a regular time or place where the children know not to disturb you unless there's an emergency.

Date evenings, weekends away, country walks, starting a hobby or interest together, meals with friends or cosy suppers a deux where you talk and are interested in each other's lives are all ways to continue supporting and investing in your relationship. Plan for the future, the times when you'll be on your own together and arrange activities; schedule a trip or organise time with friends so that there are things in the diary to look forward to.

- **The house is so quiet now!** Many people find that waking up or coming home to an empty, quiet house is one of the most difficult things to get used to once the children have left home. Change your perspective and start to regard these quiet times as a gift, a special reward for all the years of hard work and being in constant demand.

Enjoy the extra space and maybe claim a spare room as a study or studio. Invite guests to stay over at times and enjoy using your home in different ways. Use modern technology to keep in regular touch with your children. Social media, texting and video links all facilitate communications to almost anywhere in the world, possibly resulting in you enjoying better quality contact than you did when they were grumpy teenagers living at home.

- **I've so much time on my hands.** Many of us define ourselves through our role in life, our title, work, the valuable contribution we've made as a parent, provider; juggling all those responsibilities with little thought for ourselves. Once the children leave home it can provide an opportunity to reconsider our role and our occupation. If we originally left work to become a full-time parent and raise a family, reclaiming our old career may no longer be a viable option for many reasons.

  But maybe we don't need to earn as much money now that the pressure to provide and finance a family has been reduced. Now could be the time to do something that brings new meaning and satisfaction to our lives, like forging a different role, function or career. Perhaps take the opportunity to set up a business, work in charity, retrain or commit to doing something on a part-time basis. Some people choose to travel more or develop the skills and talents they were previously too busy to entertain.

The time when your children leave home can provide a valuable opportunity to re-evaluate your life. Just as they are starting a new phase in their life, so can you too use this as the perfect time to reflect on your potential, consider what you want from your relationship and focus on your quality of life; you can start to determine where you want to go from here.

Stress and the Graduate Trainee

Gaining a position as a management or business trainee is an exciting time for a new graduate trainee, full of anticipation for the opportunities that lie ahead. Working for a Merchant Bank, Investment Bank or large institution can feel like an important first step on the ladder to success. This opportunity often generates a desire to justify the faith shown in appointing them, plus a determination to demonstrate their competency.

Gradually the reality of their new life dawns as they discover that they often have to work long, stressful hours, sometimes six or seven days a week, often being thrown in at the deep end, required to find solutions to problems on their own and demonstrate a high degree of resourcefulness. The stress of these situations can at times become overwhelming.

When a person lives in a permanent state of stress they often lose their enthusiasm and motivation, become irritable, anxious, unable to relax, sleep or enjoy life. Their general health can deteriorate as their immune system becomes depleted. Stress, burnout and stress-related illnesses are a major factor in sick leave from work as people become more vulnerable to germs, infection and general malaise.

Let's look at the most effective ways for the graduate trainee to learn to manage stress and stay well:

- **Have a positive attitude** and regard being a trainee as a short-term apprenticeship. The sacrifices can be viewed as part of the learning process, the foundation stone of an exciting career and as such an invaluable opportunity to learn a lot quickly.

- **Take opportunities to cultivate allies,** a mentor or an advisor. If help is offered be gracious and accept it. If help is needed be sensible and ask for it. Be honest in admitting if a mistake has been made. It demonstrates integrity whilst allowing for things to be quickly rectified.

- **Make notes when being given information.** They can serve as an invaluable aide memoir when performing tasks for the first time. Lists are a great way of ensuring that outstanding items are not forgotten. Making a list is a useful way of keeping a clearer mind, as important things don't need to be stored in your head.

- **Pick work friends wisely.** Avoid gossip or being negative about others. Remember that each person is there to further their own career, so be circumspect in your use of critical or loose chatter.

- **Take care to look after yourself.** Organise food shopping and meals in advance so that healthy food is readily available. Try to keep fresh fruit and vegetable options handy rather than snacking on junk food and sugary treats. Minimise coffee and other stimulants whilst in the midst of intensive periods of work. They provide artificial highs and accentuate stress on the body.

- **Organise your clothes in advance.** Some people find it helpful to plan their wardrobe the night before to ensure that getting up in the morning is straightforward and free from stress. Keeping your wardrobe simple can be a help; so for example, regularly wearing black may be a way to make life less complicated.

- **Try to exercise** as often as possible. Yoga and stretching before bed can be a useful part of your wind down routine. Try to schedule in pleasant exercise if possible; a walk in the park, a few lengths of the swimming pool, a body conditioning or zumba class are all fun ways to take a healthy break from the stress of work. Plan some fun use of time on days off.

- **Sleep is especially important** during periods of intensive work and stress. Keep the bedroom clear of clutter and work related material. Quality sleep provides the best way to recharge batteries and return to work feeling refreshed. Try to relax each night before bed. Listen to pleasant music, read something light-hearted, switch off for a while.

- **Take regular breaks**. It's a fact that people perform better after taking a break from their work; a water break, a little healthy food or a walk outside can provide time to detach, clear your mind and consequently help to manage stress.

- **Practise self-hypnosis** and power napping. Self-hypnosis techniques, positive affirmations and scheduled breaks from work can help to raise your mood, keep better focus and minimise stressful responses.

And if at some point it becomes apparent that this is not the life for you there is no shame in moving onto another career. Be positive about having had a go whilst looking for something that suits you better.

Ways to Communicate Better with Family Members

Family are often our toughest critics and yet if someone from outside the family attacked us or voiced their disapproval they would rapidly change their stance and become our staunchest allies. Families can sometimes struggle to demonstrate their support on a day-to-day basis, but will often rally when they are needed.

Let's look at ways to improve communication with our family:

- Family relationships can be a minefield. On a day-to-day basis our family should be all about a comfortable, safe home. Hopefully there is security, support, companionship and an easy familiarity where one can relax and be oneself. But equally family can be cruel. Brothers and sisters may struggle to get along. Parents may treat their children badly, talk to them in a harsh or dismissive way. And often family members become invisible to each other as individuals; they become simply 'the children', 'your mummy or daddy' or 'my folks'.

- Respect can be an area that needs attention. It can be easy to ridicule or be disrespectful when we know people really well. Having lived in close proximity it can become almost automatic to laugh off their fears and concerns and not fully appreciate the situations that cause them anxiety. Pausing for a moment to check our responses can help us become more insightful, respectful and sensitive. This change in attitude often results in more positive relationships and communications with family members.

- Advice is often an area that requires sensitivity. It's not uncommon for family members to feel that they are uniquely placed to freely dispense their comments, advice and criticisms without a second thought. Waiting until asked or tactfully picking a time when the subject is being discussed can be a more appropriate and respectful way of offering advice.

- The harsh reality is that our family members know us better than anyone. They are only too aware of the horror stories in our past, the times when we made a fool of ourselves or committed some embarrassing folly. They know the anecdotes that we wish could be forgotten and as such have the power to remind us of them if they choose. Consigning those stories to times when they make appropriate listening, times when you're sharing affectionate reminiscences is a more sensitive way to communicate within the family.

- Family members can fail to register how far we've come, how much we've grown and developed or be able to appreciate our many successes and accomplishments. They may still see us as the awkward child, struggling teenager or young apprentice. They may not value our achievements in the same way that others might. Seeing each other as the world does can revise our appreciation of each other and inject respect into the way we communicate with each other.

- Reunions and family events can sometimes be difficult and require a certain amount of diplomacy as estranged relatives meet and either try to avoid each other or compete in an effort to demonstrate how much more successful/popular they are than others in the group. Being tactful and good-humoured can be a strain, but remembering that this is a rare occurrence can help. A good survival trick is to pretend you're at a business meeting where good manners and best behaviour come automatically. Adopting that approach can be a way to successfully survive an unpleasant or infrequent reunion.

Some families love spending time with each other, they speak to each other regularly and love to keep each other updated with their news. For others, family relationships are more stressful and need treating with a degree of caution. Whoever we're with, family, friends, colleagues, it's important to treat people as we'd like to be treated, with respect, good manners and appreciation of them as individuals in their own right. That way we find that our communications and relationships improve and become more meaningful.

The Problem with Family Holidays

Sharing holidays with our extended family, our brothers, sisters, parents or in-laws, can seem in principle to be an excellent idea. The expenses are shared, children will be looked after by a trustworthy group of loving family members and companionship is readily available. Mealtimes become sociable occasions and there may well be enough people in the group to accommodate everyone's different choices for activities.

The reality is often more stressful. In-laws may be seen as difficult, judgemental, critical, possessive or controlling. Sometimes in-laws and their enforced new family can find it unpleasant to be in close proximity for extended periods of time. The related son or daughter can end up feeling like a piggy in the middle, trying to keep the peace and negotiate a middle ground between parents and spouse.

In-laws can be a major source of strife in a marriage. We tolerate our own family's foibles and annoying eccentricities, but there may be things about our partner's family that cause irritation and discomfort at times. Successful relationships require give and take, the ability to compromise, exercise tolerance and hopefully retain a sense of humour and perspective.

Let's look at some of the stresses of family holidays and explore ways to minimise them:

- Instead of sharing the same apartment or villa might it be more sensible to book separate accommodation for each group? That way you can spend pre-arranged time together with comfortable alone time afterwards. Living under each other's noses, especially in self-catering accommodation can be stifling at times, as niggles about food, eating habits, children's bedtime, bathroom rotas and chores start to surface.

- An activity holiday can be stressful for some people. If your partner cannot ski, play golf, horse ride or is not as energetic as the rest of the family it can provide an additional reason for their discomfort. Compromise might involve your partner availing themselves of the opportunity to remedy their lack of skill during the holiday. By booking skiing or riding lessons it could provide a solution to several problems; they would get a break from the main group for a while, have some respite from the intensity of the family interactions and have a valuable opportunity to learn or improve a particular skill.

- By showing some initiative your partner can take responsibility for their happiness on the holiday. Booking lessons or choosing activities they like the sound of shows a desire to participate and improve the quality of their holiday. They may enjoy their choices whilst demonstrating to you and your family that they're willing to make an effort. Reciprocation and appreciation are an important way of reassuring your partner that you value the effort they are making, as is arranging to spend some of the holiday having fun together.

- Doing something away from the main group provides everyone with alternative topics of conversation when the time comes to eventually meet up again. Also, being occupied elsewhere dilutes the intensity of being constantly in each other's company and allows the time you do spend together to be more fun, relaxed and interesting.

- When we're the partner, the in-law, taking control of some of the decisions that affect us and the way we spend our holiday can help us to feel more positive. By choosing to participate and be involved we become more proactive and enthusiastic. Rather than feeling neglected, frustrated or miserable through sitting around, waiting for people to return from their happy, exciting activities, instead it's far better to enter into the spirit of things on our own terms.

And then, when the time comes for us to need our partner's support, perhaps at a family occasion or when we would value their attendance at something important he or she is far more likely to reciprocate with enthusiasm and return our generous support.

Ways to Reduce the Stress of Christmas

The Archbishop of Canterbury made headlines in 2014 when he aired his views on the stress that many of us inflict on ourselves at Christmas. His concerns were the amount of debt and the pressure to create the perfect Christmas that many of us subject ourselves to. All too often the pressure causes irritability, arguments and stress, contributing to real problems in relationships.

With many of us working long hours, perhaps coping as single parents, we're keen to make Christmas extra-special. Often there's a perception that everyone else is enjoying the idealised, magazine and media-promoted perfect Christmas; the one where everyone enjoys each other's company and all is well with the world. There may be a hope that if we act as if everything's fine it will make it so. The desire to conceal the true state of our less than perfect lives may also be a factor.

But there are some great ways to help reduce festive stress:

- Talk to your children. Perhaps introduce the idea of them receiving one main present and other smaller gifts. Explain a little of the pressure you're under. Children are often able to understand and be reasonable if they're talked to properly.

- Consider giving your children memories rather than actual gifts; taking them out for a day, having an indoor picnic, spending fun time together pursuing activities can all make Christmas special, enhance your relationship and let them have something really precious, your time.

- List in advance the people who you want to buy Christmas presents for, with a price limit and suggestions next to each name. This avoids aimlessly wandering around stores, with the resultant last-minute panic buying.

- Suggest a nominal price limit per gift, especially for adults; then everyone has to use their imagination as they shop. Maybe decide on one present per person for a Secret Santa with everyone getting a token present. Many people express relief when someone suggests this option. Don't forget how many of those fabulously extravagant gifts are unwanted or unappreciated and often get returned after the holidays.

- Use local Christmas markets, craft fairs, privately owned shops to find unusual, original gifts that have no obvious price tag attached to them. It can be lovely to give and receive a gift that is unique and purchased especially with the recipient in mind.

- Wait until nearer to Christmas to shop, if possible. Many shops start their sales during the week before Christmas. Often good value purchases can be made at that time.

- Select a significant photograph and have it beautifully framed, making a thoughtful, personalised gift. Or utilise your talents: bake a delicious cake, arrange lovely seasonal flowers, paint a picture and give a personalised, individual gift.

- How about babysitting vouchers? They are priceless and most parents will appreciate the opportunity for an evening out, leaving their children safely in the care of someone they know and trust. Or offer practical help with gardening, de-cluttering, decorating.

- Reduce the expense of entertaining by making a hot-pot supper, a chilli, a lasagne with garlic bread and all the trimmings. With so much rich food over Christmas, a simple, tasty casserole is often very welcome. Or arrange a safari dinner where one course is served at each person's house. It can be fun to walk from one house to the next and saves on expense and effort.

- If you're anticipating a houseful of guests over the holidays it's worth planning ahead, drawing up menus, batch cooking in advance, planning some days where a hot-pot supper or chilli will be a less expensive and welcome alternative to the rich food and banqueting.

- Share the load. Ask people to bring their signature dish, provide an item or a bottle or two. Delegate duties like setting the table, preparing the vegetables, washing up. That way you may even have time for a relaxing bath and be also able to have fun yourself on the day.

- If you're on your own why not make the most of having a free day or two. Plan treats for yourself. Have a lie in, cook your favourite meals, organise some trips out, note the films you want to watch, spend time reading a special book or have a leisurely bath with candles.

  Also be ready to accept invitations. Other people may be so preoccupied with their own situation that they don't fully appreciate that you're on your own. If you get invited somewhere really consider accepting the offer. You may be perfectly fine on your own, but sometimes it is good to make the effort, move out of your familiar environment and try something new. You never know, it may result in a new friendship or an unexpectedly pleasant afternoon.

- Source free events like carol services or plan indoor activities like board games, charades, or quizzes. They can provide a welcome break from the hours of television repeats! Outdoor activities can include a brisk country walk or team sports like football or rounders. Inexpensive, fun ways to burn off energy and enjoy Christmas.

- Let the children help and ask them to plan one day each over the school holidays. They are often surprisingly creative. Older children may even enjoy the opportunity to work to a budget and organise the finer details, an interesting and educational exercise for them.

A little forward planning can reduce the stress and expense of this time of the year. By being organised, sharing jobs, planning menus, batch cooking in advance, scheduling in some 'me' time, Christmas can be a special time for everyone, including yourself. And, even if things don't go to plan, the slip ups and mishaps often become the stuff of family legend and humorous anecdotes, remembered with affection over many forthcoming years.

The Best Way to Support Our Parents as They Get Older

There comes a time when we suddenly start to notice that our parents are getting older. Things that they used to do with ease start to become a chore, get left undone or no longer provide the pleasure that they used to. The garden may become untended, the house not as clean or spending time with the grandchildren is obviously becoming more of an effort.

Staying active and engaged in life is crucial to physical and mental health and well-being and there are many sensitive and supportive ways to share quality time with our parents whilst still enjoying the valuable time we have left with them.

Let's look at some ways to support our parents as they age, as their situation changes and they start to realise their vulnerabilities:

- **Exercise** is an important part of keeping fit and active, but needs to be modified as a person becomes less flexible and energetic. Many gyms and local authorities offer classes for the older person. They are a source of companionship as well *as* providing a regular reason to get out of the house and make an effort. Yoga, Pilates and Tai Chi are viable options that enhance core stability and flexibility.

Within a family going for a walk can be a time to catch up and enjoy each other's company whilst providing an opportunity for some gentle exercise. Parks often have fairly even surfaces for walking, provide regular seating and, by including afternoon tea, make a pleasant way to spend an afternoon together.

Organised senior walking groups often meet in the week, undertake a moderate walk and then have refreshments. It can be a welcome way to spend a few hours mid-week whilst providing an opportunity to mix and meet with similar people and make time for social contact.

- **Social engagements** provide fun and a reason to look after themselves, dress smartly and take a pride in their appearance. Having a reason to get dressed up and go out for a meal or to see a show or concert is a fun way to spend time. Keeping a look out for things that they might enjoy and informing them about plays, concerts, musicals or exhibitions that would appeal can make our parent's social life more enjoyable. Nostalgia, choosing shows from when they were young can prompt reminiscences, conversations and happy memories.

- **Mental activity** is important to keep their minds exercised and alert. Sudoku puzzles and crosswords appear in daily newspapers. When I visit my mother we tend to have a game of Scrabble. I don't let her win and it's always a fight to the end! It's become our little ritual; we have a coffee, a Tia Maria and a game of Scrabble.

Social groups can provide opportunities to keep mentally active. Learning to play bridge, joining bingo sessions or attending talks and lectures on interesting topics can provide interest and stimulus. Also if reading is tiring many libraries provide audiobooks, often narrated by famous actors. Many people like to listen to those whilst on holiday, relaxing on the beach.

- **A little support** in the home can ease the burden for elderly folk. Getting someone in to help with the cleaning, to do the heavy gardening or provide support with shopping or cooking can make all the difference to their quality of life. There are now many companies that provide different menus of care options, available to people who prefer to remain in their homes, but need a little extra help. Often older people want to stay in their own home for as long as they can. A little support with the more difficult jobs can enable that to happen.

'Tips for remaining in your own home in later life' is covered in the 'Home' chapter of the book.

Should We Talk About Death and Dying?

Many of us fear talking about death and dying. It's often regarded as one of those 'unmentionables'; distasteful, not appropriate to discuss in public, insensitive. And yet in some cultures death is regarded as simply the next phase of life's journey, something that we move into once our reason for being here on earth is over.

What is it that causes so much apprehension in talking about death and dying?

- To talk about death means acknowledging our own mortality and that can be unnerving. We may even fear that by discussing death we are tempting fate and drawing it closer to us. For many people death is something that they don't want to think about; it happens to other people, old people, someone else.

- The unknown is a significant concern when reflecting on death. Even people who believe in God often have apprehensions and questions which remain a matter of faith and trust. We may say that we believe in life after death, but many people keep their fingers crossed at the same time. And yet, talking about death and dying can bring much peace and comfort to everyone involved in the discussion.

- Often people can feel guilty and unsure as to what their loved one wanted after their death. Talking about death and dying in a relaxed way allows people to ask questions, to say things they need to say and discuss how they feel.

- Discovering what loved ones want, their wishes if they become seriously ill, their final intentions after they have gone can support a more comfortable atmosphere for everyone involved.

- It can be helpful to clear the air of grievances, if there's an opportunity to do so. Talking things through in a non-acrimonious way can allow people to understand each other's point of view, even if resolution or mutual agreement does not occur.

- Discussing death and dying whilst of an age when it's probably not an imminent prospect, and is able to be discussed intelligently, is often a good time for this to happen. It's important to be sensitive if initiating this conversation with someone elderly or who is seriously ill.

- If that's the case it's usually best to wait for the other person to raise the subject, perhaps when they've referred to what they want to happen after they've gone. This can provide an opportunity to follow-up on their comments with a sensitive, respectful conversation about their thoughts, things they'd like to happen and allay concerns they might have. This can bring peace, comfort and reassurance to all concerned.

CHAPTER SIX

Stress and Home

The Best Way to Make a House a Home

Many busy people find that without even noticing how it happened, their home has become somewhere they solely use to sleep, change their clothes and occasionally eat. Teenagers are notorious for treating their home like a hotel, turning up whenever they need feeding, want something or have nowhere else to go. But even when we're exceptionally busy, we can still attend to all those commitments and responsibilities as well as establish a home where we go to feel safe, relax and be ourselves.

Let's look at some ways to invest in our homes:

- Time needs to be committed initially. It can take time to find the best place to live, somewhere that feels comfortable, is convenient for work, supports the children's lives, is near to family and friends and at the same time is affordable. If any of these elements are missing, living there can become a source of stress and resentment. And once we've found our future home, time needs to be spent in making the place suitable; organizing the rooms and deciding on any alterations that may be needed in order to make it comfortable.

- Creativity can make our home unique, special and showcase our personality. Choosing colours, fabrics and decor can be both a daunting and exciting experience, certainly the first time. Discovering what works and what doesn't work can provide an interesting lesson. Some people enjoy working on their home themselves. They relish the feeling of satisfaction that comes from having made the effort and invested of themselves. Other people prefer to instruct professionals and avoid the mess, turning up to appreciate the end result.

- Children often enjoy being allowed to decorate their bedrooms in their own way. It's not uncommon, after a divorce, for children to be given creative licence to decorate their bedrooms in their two homes. It enables them to feel that they have a permanent presence with both parents.

- It's important to continuously give attention to our home. We feel more committed to a place when we look after it, maintain it and spend quality time there. Keeping our home clean and fresh, updating its look by occasionally buying new things, fresh flowers, pretty cushions or a new picture, demonstrates that we care and like to treat it with affection.

- Company and friendship adds to our home's ambiance. Inviting people round for drinks, a bite of supper, a game of cards or a girly pamper evening can mean that we are motivated to keep our place tidy and are happy to share it with others. Opening our doors and being hospitable means that we are inviting people to get to know us better. We are letting them into our personal space.

- Sharing fun and laughter benefits the atmosphere at home. Many of us are able to sense very quickly if we visit a house that is unloved or has an unhappy story to tell. When children feel settled and allowed to invite friends round to play it makes for a relaxed home. New mothers can sometimes feel isolated, especially if they have taken a break from their careers and haven't yet made friends with their neighbours or other local mothers. Tentatively building friendships by inviting other mums round for a coffee and a chat can make life a little easier, whilst also sharing companionship, fun and advice. When home provides a welcome to visitors it makes for a more comfortable, friendly place.

It can take a little while, but home gradually becomes a place where we look forward to spending time, a haven where we're happy to return. It's important to be able to relax and be ourselves when we're there, whether we're on our own or with others, happy and content to enjoy our personal place.

Ways to Relax at Home

But in order to relax at home there are a few basic ground rules that are useful to consider:

- Learn to leave the regular stresses of the day behind you, rather than bring them home. If you have several areas of tension outside the home, perhaps to do with work, friends or family, try to find ways to draw a line under them until the next time you're required to deal with them. It may be a useful suggestion to go to the gym after work, to park your car and listen to music or to use the drive home as a way to mentally unwind.

- If there are serious family or work-related matters that are affecting you, which you feel need to be discussed at home, set aside a time which is convenient for everyone. Allow enough time to properly talk things through. Then, once the discussion is over, tell yourself that you've done all you can for now and set the problems to one side. It's counter-productive to continuously re-hash them. Agree to follow-up with some quiet time, where everyone's able to relax and de-stress.

- If there are home-related issues and problems, agree not to discuss potentially volatile subjects after a certain time, say 9 pm. No one benefits from a late-night ruckus after which everyone goes to bed feeling stressed or unhappy. When there's a need to discuss difficult family-related matters, like the children's behaviour, or the in-laws, pick a time which is suitable for everyone. Then matters can hopefully be dealt with and resolved in one sitting.

- Ensure that every evening is not spent doing chores. Some people find that batch-cooking each week's meals at the weekend is a way of providing more free time in the week. Then meals simply need to be re-heated each evening. For some people paying for help with the ironing or cleaning is worth the expense; they'd rather pay someone else and be able to relax and enjoy their free time.

- If you maintain the house yourself, be reasonable about needing everywhere to be squeaky clean. Yes, it's important to have the chores done and the place tidy and inviting, but being too fixated may need a little negotiation, especially if there are other stresses and pressures in your life. Sometimes it's healthier to go for a walk in the country and relax rather than spend the day polishing the windows or the furniture.

- Ask everyone in the family to suggest ideas for ways they'd like to share time together. They may suggest playing board games, watching films whilst eating popcorn, cooking a meal, baking cakes, or spending time in the garden. Work through the list and allow each person's ideas to be acted upon.

- Make sure to use colour. Inject lots of personality in the form of artwork, cushions, bright fabrics and prints. Change your paintings and colour scheme occasionally to keep your home fresh and vibrant. Personal touches can make all the difference to your home and don't need to cost a lot of money.

- Music is important. It brings its own mood and can help support relaxation and letting go of stress. Music can set the right tone for eating, chatting, having a long leisurely bath or simply doing nothing and making the most of a little personal space. Play music in the evenings or on a free afternoon and enjoy the opportunity to work your way through your music catalogue.

- Sit down together to eat. Many families tend to cater for individual meals, eat separately and hardly ever sit down together. If it's not practical to eat together every night, try to get agreement to sit down together for a family meal at least one evening a week or on a Sunday. Talking together over dinner helps a family stay connected, up-to-date with each other's news and helps to form closer bonds.

- Schedule breaks. Whatever you're doing, aim to work for a time and then allow yourself a break for a drink, time in the garden or for reading a book. Working from home doesn't provide the designated breaks that working in an office does. It can be tempting to do just one more task when we're at home. Stop after each main task and commit to a treat and a relaxing break.

- Invite friends round for an hour. That way you have to stop and relax. And having guests is a great way of sharing your home and keeping in touch with the outside world.

- Be disciplined about keeping on top of filing and paperwork. Read and file your post as it arrives and dispose of mailshots and items that you don't need. This helps you to keep on top of your admin, helps you to manage stress and helps to keep your home tidy.

- Book yourself in your diary. Plan an afternoon to yourself for a long leisurely bath or to watch your favourite film. Or book a massage or a treatment at home and enjoy the fact that they're coming to you; you can relax afterwards. Turn the phone off, avoid distractions and allow yourself some quiet time to enjoy your home for a couple of hours.

- Arrange for the children to be picked up from school by a friend and maybe even have a sleepover for the night. You can do this for each other, say once a month. Then you can enjoy the freedom of knowing that you don't have to rush around after them for once. Avoid the temptation to use all the time catching up on chores. Maybe do a couple of important things, then relax and have a pleasant evening doing very little.

- Make your bedroom an oasis of calm. Keep electrical gadgets to a minimum and screen off any work areas, so keeping the main bedroom your special place of peace and relaxation. Scented candles, relaxing music and clean sheets all add to the delicious ambiance.

- Relax outside in your garden area. Whether it be a patio, an orchard or a window box, try to have an area that requires minimal effort to maintain. Enjoy relaxing outside in nature. Feed the birds and encourage them to come to your garden so that you can enjoy their singing and nest-building throughout the year. Sit and read a book in the afternoon sunshine or simply doze for an hour or so. Yet another lovely way to relax at home!

Try to establish your home as calm and comfortable place to relax. Some people look forward to their annual holiday as a time when they completely relax and de-stress, but waiting for an annual break can seem a long way off. With a little planning, forethought and help it's possible for your home to become a haven where you relax and recharge your batteries on a daily basis.

De-clutter and Freshen up Your Life

Some people are ruthless at clearing out their clutter. I have a friend who is so strict with herself that on occasion she has had to return to the charity shop to buy back items she has donated to them. Too late she realises that she still needs something she has previously discarded.

Many of us are not so rigorous with our possessions. Some of us will have seen the TV programmes, where people have hoarded so much that they find it difficult to even enter their homes. But it's important at times to take stock, sort out our stuff and de-clutter. Let's look at why:

- Clutter can block your energy flow and make progress difficult. Just think about someone who has a messy desk or an overflowing in-tray. Often they haven't a clue as to where to start or what to tackle first. They pick up one thing, then another but feel overwhelmed as to where to begin making inroads into their tasks. Introducing order can help with prioritising and feeling more in control. De-cluttering helps ensure clearer, more efficient thought processes.

- Hording clothes can be tempting. Few people wear their clothes, shoes and accessories to destruction; in fact it's estimated that we wear only 10-20% of what's in our wardrobes. Many people prefer to wear items that are new, fresh and fashionable and so they top-up their wardrobe regularly. Discarding items that are dated, the wrong size or out of favour can be hard to do, but before you restock it's important to sort through your existing items in a realistic way. It can be tempting to argue that your older pieces will eventually come back into fashion or that you will lose weight and be able to fit into some of your favourite outfits but, deep down you know that it's unlikely to happen.

  Some people find that a twelve month rule works well; if something hasn't been worn within the last year they let it go. By deciding to donate unwanted items to a second-hand/pre-loved/antique/charity shop you can either earn yourself some money or help your favourite charity. And clearing out your drawers and cupboards provides the space for newer clothing to be more easily seen and thus more likely to be worn.

- Possessions can have sentimental associations. Children may have given you precious handmade, pottery dishes and bric-a-brac over the years. But gradually your home can become full of too much clutter and in need of some fairly ruthless intervention. Take photographs of your sentimental items and include them in a scrapbook of your treasures. Children's artwork could be photographed and made into a photobook. Then you can let them go. You're able to keep a memory of special items without the need to fill your home with lots of stuff.

People with cluttered bedrooms often benefit from improved sleep after a serious tidy-up session. Your bedroom really ought to be spacious and airy. And for those people who use their bedrooms as an office, complete with workstation, computer and files, try screening off that section. Defining each area helps your room feel more organised and less cluttered.

Many homes have a spare bedroom, attic or garage that over the years becomes full of unwanted clutter that they don't want to part with 'just yet'. Often the piles of 'stuff' get added to, without ever being revisited. I knew someone years ago who couldn't bear to throw anything away. Things had become so bad that he regularly added to his hoard by raiding rubbish skips and junk shops. He couldn't bear the thought of missing out on something that he felt would be really useful in the future.

But he had so much stuff that he could never locate an item when it was needed. Whenever that happened he had to go out and buy new. We worked on his issues and negotiated a better solution, where he became comfortable about giving items away when he felt sure that they were going to a good home. Another option are the many free recycling websites which are available to rehome the items we no longer want but could be of use to someone else.

- De-cluttering on your own can take a long time, as it can be tempting to stop and go through each item individually. It can be all too easy to become absorbed in the memories that each item evokes. I suggest to my clients that they start small, take their time and tackle one drawer at a time, so that they don't become overwhelmed and lose heart.

   Or it can be useful to enlist the help of a tough friend or hire the services of a professional de-clutterer, who will help you blitz the mess in stages. Another option can be to follow the lead of a friend of mine, who hires a skip twice a year to help her stay on top of her clutter.

Enjoy Your Garden and Improve Your Health

Many people find that choosing a house with a garden is a significant consideration when they're looking to buy a new home. The thought of pottering about, tending to flower beds, sitting out in the sunshine, having a barbecue with friends and generally spending time in their garden appeals to many people.

Let's look at some of the benefits of enjoying time in your garden:

- Looking after the garden is a great form of exercise. Bending to weed, stretching to trim high branches, using equipment to dig, prune and rake all require strength, flexibility and a good hand grip. Often you'll walk several times around the garden without even realising, perhaps pushing a wheelbarrow or cutting back shrubs. These activities all stimulate the heart and lungs into sustaining a reasonable level of physical activity. The good thing is this exercise can be done at one's own pace, at a level that is comfortable for each individual's fitness and capability.

- Fresh air and spending time in the garden is a positive commitment to good health and wellbeing. It can be fascinating to see the different wildlife in one's garden; birds, bees, butterflies, squirrels, as well as more exotic creatures like toads, foxes and bats that you can often spot. And often a day spent gardening results in a healthy appetite followed by a good night's sleep.

- Stimulating one's senses is important. Sitting for hours at a desk, on a computer or behind a wheel or evenings spent watching television are regular everyday experiences for many of us. So going outdoors and using your imagination and creativity to reflect on different ways to transform your garden is a great way to de-stress. You experience the different seasons, enjoy nature, get to feel the earth in your hands, breathe fresh air and enjoy the many colours, shades, smells and sounds of the outdoors. Gardening can be a great sensory experience.

- Gardening is a good way to engage children or other family members and can provide an interesting, ongoing joint project. Children love being muddy, they enjoy planting and watering their little patch of vegetables, tomatoes or strawberries, rushing out each day to monitor their progress. It's a good way to capture their attention and teach them about nature without them necessarily realising that they're learning.

- Allotments are popular in the UK; these are additional plots of land available to rent, usually located away from the home, where people cultivate extra produce, often for their own consumption. Eating home-grown fruit and vegetables can make good economic sense, provide healthy seasonal crops and make for especially tasty and satisfying mealtimes.

- But some people prefer their garden to be low maintenance. Installing decking or a patio with flower tubs can reduce the amount of maintenance required to keep it tidy. Adding tubs of ready grown plants can turn a garden into an array of colour and fragrance overnight. Some people add gravel or wood chippings to their flower beds to prevent the growth of weeds or they may even lay artificial grass to remove the need for mowing. But, for many the attraction of a garden is tending it, getting one's hands dirty through weeding, pruning and nurturing it.

- An attractive garden can add an extra room to the home, an area where you can entertain and invite friends round for a barbecue or picnic. Or you could sit quietly and enjoy relaxing, reading a book or watching the children play in safety. Even monitoring the growth of plants in your window box can bring pleasure to your home. Enjoy your garden, whether it be big or small.

The Importance of Pets

Some people feel that a house is not a home until there is an animal comfortably in residence, but pets are a huge responsibility; there is the expense of feeding and healthcare, the attention they need on a daily basis, concerns about what to do with them whenever you go away and finally old age and end of life considerations.

Also, pets are quite independent and come with their own agenda. Whether you be rich or poor, king or pauper, a pet is oblivious to all of that and will simply treat you as it sees fit. My experiences have been with stray animals, dogs and cats, all of whom have been demanding but have added significantly to my life.

What is it about pets and why are they so important to us?

- They need looking after. Pets rely on us for their food, warmth and safety. No matter how we're feeling we have to get up, get out of bed and tend to their needs. Someone I know who had a long-term debilitating condition, found that her symptoms improved when she got a dog. The responsibility meant that she had to regularly let him out into the garden, feed him and interact with him. His companionship made her more alert and engaged in life and she found it easier to make an effort and become more active.

- They are demanding. Many of us spend more time trying to choose the 'right' pet food for our beloved animals than we do for ourselves. I regularly join several other animal owners in the pet food aisles, trying to determine which brand and flavour they're going to deign to eat this week. We might roll our eyes with mock frustration, but it's a situation that we undertake with love, humour and commitment.

- They are welcoming. How lovely is it to come home when there are animals waiting! There is a definite requirement not to leave them too long, but it's also a pleasure to come home when we're looking forward to seeing our pets again. Single people sometimes delay coming home when they live alone, but if they have pets there is a compelling reason to return home and feed or walk them and enjoy their companionship.

- Life is put into better perspective. Priorities change when you realise that you can't move because a purring cat is on your knee or a dog is lying across your feet. Somehow the day's stresses and irritations fade and become calmer when you're taking your dog for a long walk or are concerned about the health of your cat. And other considerations are put into a different order. Anyone with animals will recognise the times when they're getting ready to go out, only to discover animal hair on their lovely new outfit, or the fruitless search for a missing shoe that eventually turns up in the dog's bed! All you can do is ruefully smile, dust yourself off and promise yourself to be more careful next time.

Animals are a valuable addition to our lives. They teach us about patience, love, companionship and responsibility. They depend on us for their quality of life and enhance ours so much in return. It's devastating when they eventually die but it's important to treasure the gift of our time together. The memories and anecdotes can stay with us all our lives.

Photographs Can Make Your House a Home

Making the transition from house to home means introducing personal touches. It can be little things, like a collection of pebbles and shells that were found on a special holiday beach, a bowl made in junior school by one of the children or finger paintings stuck on the fridge door. These are the touches that make all the difference, that make a house a home, mainly because all these items have their own stories to tell. They reference the family's growth and are often the items that guests and visitors want to know about, to discover who made them, where they came from, what's their story.

Photographs can be an important part of our emotional investment in our home, because even if we move, wherever we live we can take them with us. It's easy to carry our significant photographs with us and feel connected to our family and friends. Displaying framed photographs can immediately lay claim to a new space, which is why many people like to show them at the office, on their desk or at times when they travel away and are living in hotel rooms.

Whether they be amateur or professional, our photographs are a pictorial log of our life and the lives of those who are important to us. They can remind us of happy times from long ago, of people no longer with us and unattractive ones can motivate us to take charge of ourselves and do something positive like lose weight or update our image. Amateur photographs are commonplace these days and are often taken as selfies, using mobile phones. They're fun, natural and document our daily lives, often being loaded onto social media.

Our first experience of a professional photographer may have been at school, from the awkward individual shots, dutifully sent out to relatives at Christmas, right through to the large annual 'class of' school assembly. Over the years official family photographs regularly document the significant events, like graduations, engagements or to record a new family group. Professional photographers are often booked for weddings, to record new babies, a significant birthday or anniversary and also for corporate business events.

The professional photographs are often the ones that are beautifully framed and hung on the walls or are displayed proudly around our rooms. They often provide a focal point in a room, so making the room a comfortable family place. They portray the people and places that have a special significance in the household.

People are often attracted to the photographs when they first enter a room. They can prompt interesting conversations; about the fashions, discussions about the different people featured, the stories attached to the photographs, why the picture was taken. They may prompt nostalgia and sentimental anecdotes about the people who featured in our lives and add sentiment and emotional context to our home.

The Subtle Power of Sound in Our Lives

Many of us live in a world of constant noise. Noise pollution is becoming a cause for concern in many people's lives, from noisy neighbours, other travellers on public transport and the stress of working in open-plan offices. It's interesting that many supermarkets have stopped using background music as they began to discover that many customers found it irritating and stressful.

But sound and noise can convey information in perhaps unconsidered ways. Our senses hold a database of accumulated experiences relating to all our senses including sound. These memories can be good or bad, evocative of people, times and associations from our past. These sounds wield a subtle power in our lives.

How many of us have become affectionately nostalgic over tunes from our youth when unexpectedly heard on the radio, as we reminisce over people, places and things that were in our lives back then? Conversely, the tone in a complete stranger's voice can make us tense, angry, defensive, even fearful, as their words, tone and demeanour trigger memories of a long forgotten, unpleasant time in our lives. Or we may find a stranger to be comforting and reassuring as they unconsciously remind us of a supportive teacher, neighbour or family friend.

Other sounds often cause a more universal reaction; the grating of chalk on a board makes many people cringe. A child laughing, someone giggling uncontrollably, a champagne cork popping, the sound of the sea, bird song, church bells ringing are sounds that often make people smile, feel secure and able to relax - unless those sounds have a past negative experience connected to them.

So, when we're looking to make our home comfortable and free from stress it's important that we consider the sounds we introduce and permit in our home. Do we want the radio, TV or music to be automatically turned on whenever we enter our home, or is there a relevance to sometimes enjoying the quiet of a silent home? Do we want our children to be regularly watching and listening to the noisy barrage of their computer games? Sometimes silence or less strident sounds can bring soothing calm into our home.

Come Out of Hibernation and Enjoy Easter

For many of us Easter signifies the end of our winter mind-set, as we begin to notice the lighter mornings, longer evenings and better weather. Let's look at some ways to really kickstart the process of emerging from our hibernation after the cold days and long, 'too dark to go out' winter nights:

- Enjoy the colours around you and let them energize you. Spring flowers will by now have been in bloom for a little while, so start to enjoy the lovely colours and let them lift your spirits. Freshen up your home and introduce bright colours. Fresh flowers, cheerful additions like lighter colours and fabrics, bright cushions and pictures can all revitalise your home. Prepare your garden for planting; even a small patch can bring pleasure.

- Use Easter as a time to spring-clean. Put away your dark winter clothes and add brighter colours and touches to your wardrobe. As you change from your winter to lighter spring wardrobe, decide which items are out of date and need to be discarded. Some of those items may be of value to charity shops.

- Review your New Year's Resolutions and decide if they need to be adapted, reintroduced or amended. If you gave up something for Lent, now could be a good time to set more goals, to keep you focussed on improving your life. Renewing your commitment to improved fitness, confidence and a better quality of life is a good way to start feeling motivated for spring.

- Commit to going out as a family. Look out for special offers, as many family attractions start to open their doors again at Easter. Petting zoos, parks with animals and country walks all offer hours of free entertainment for children as they seek out the new-born ducklings, lambs and other young animals. Enjoy the outdoors as a family; play ball games, go walking or for bike rides and bring exercise, adventure and joint activities into your life, all for little or no expense.

- As the light nights return commit to becoming more active again as a person/family/couple. Winter is often a time when people come home of an evening, close the curtains and settle down in front of the television. Now that winter's over and Easter is upon us why not decide to introduce a regular stroll or meet up with friends for early supper; become more proactive, rather than waiting for someone else to make suggestions.

- If you have children studying for exams, help them manage their stress levels by providing regular breaks, opportunities for fresh air and exercise, as well as healthy snacks. An occasional distraction from work will allow them to reduce their stress levels and enable them to return to their studies re-energised and able to concentrate better.

Make the most of the coming lighter nights and warmer weather. Whether you're single, a couple or a family there is the potential now to start emerging from the winter months, enjoy the opportunity to get out and do more with the extra light hours available each day.

Tips to Enjoy a Positive Autumn

Before too long we begin to notice that the days are starting to draw in and it's taking longer in the morning for daylight to appear. We start to recognise that summer is over. People begin the countdown to Christmas and discuss whether it's too early to switch on their central heating.

But autumn can be a positive time of the year:

- Make your home a cosy haven. Focus on using luscious fabrics and warm colours like red, gold, bronze and auburn for cushions, curtains, rugs and throws. Add fragrance with scented candles, pot pourri and diffusers.

- Lighting has a major bearing on our mood, wellbeing and stress levels. Harsh light can cause stress and tension so lighting at home really needs to be soft and mellow. Lamps, side lights and candles can all be used to good effect in creating a relaxing glow. Outdoor lighting can enable you to continue using your garden over the autumn months, whilst keeping your windows clean means that they let in as much light as possible.

- Look at your music collection. How often do you play your older tracks? Invite friends round for a music evening and enjoy sharing your collection with them. It could spark off some interesting exchanges.

- Start using your slow cooker. It's great to come home to a freshly cooked meal that's ready to eat, and it often means that you eat in a less expensive, far healthier way. A little preparation means that you avoid the pre-chilled ready meal or takeaway options.

- Use opportunities to go outside and enjoy the daylight. Go outside for breaks and lunch whenever you can. Exercise outdoors. A brisk walk in the countryside or the local park can provide quality time with family or friends. Wrap up warm, then afterwards enjoy a glass of mulled wine, hot chocolate or a nourishing casserole that's been simmering slowly all day. Or you can stop to eat in a country pub and relax in front of the log fire.

- Enjoy cosy, relaxing evenings relaxing at home. Take a long leisurely bath with scented candles and the delicious bath oils you've been saving for a special occasion. Schedule an evening for catching up on your favourite films or box sets, read that book you've long been meaning to read, make those neglected catch-up phone calls or invite friends round for supper.

- Buy fresh flowers for somewhere unexpected like the landing or bathroom. They're a treat and will brighten up your home.

- Prepare your garden for autumn. Winter flowering plants bring colour so that you have a pleasant view from your window. Feed the birds regularly and enjoy seeing how many different kinds come to visit.

- Safari suppers can be a fun, inexpensive way to socialise and enjoy autumn evenings with local friends and neighbours. Each course is provided by a different person as the guests move from one house to the next throughout the meal.

- Board games can be surprisingly good fun as everyone's competitive streak emerges. Some people find that games nights become a regular part of their family time or social calendar. Record your favourite television programmes so that you can view them at your leisure.

- Painting and crafts are a good way for children to enjoy autumn afternoons indoors. Collect pine cones, leaves and grasses on nature walks and use them to make scrapbooks, pictures or even greetings and Christmas cards. Let them plan an indoor picnic and help with the preparation. It's fun to sit on a gingham tablecloth, eating sandwiches and drinking juice on the lounge or kitchen floor.

A little forethought, preparation and organisation can ensure that autumn is a cosy, relaxing and pleasant time. As the evenings begin to draw in, commit to using your home and free time well, so that whether you're alone or with others you make the most of all this season has to offer.

Is it a Good Decision to Keep the House After Our Divorce?

The house is often an emotive subject when it comes to determining who keeps what after a divorce. It's the major financial asset in most relationships, and has also been the backdrop to the family and its ongoing story. It has been home, heavily invested in over the years with love, effort, stress and tears.

Sometimes though in a divorce, it's important to stand back a little and detach emotionally whilst reviewing the situation. It can pay dividends in the future to have taken time at the outset to weigh up the various implications and practical considerations. Many major decisions need making at this vulnerable time, decisions that impact on every area of life. So taking good advice and sufficient time to make the best decision is important.

Let's look at some relevant factors to consider when deciding whether to keep the house after divorce:

- Familiarity is often important after a divorce. After such a turbulent time there can be a strong desire to quickly establish a feeling of being safe, secure and settled. Keeping life as familiar as possible can be tempting. There has been so much turmoil and change that holding onto the comfortable, familiar haven that is home can seem to be the right thing to do. Often advisers say not to make hasty decisions after a death or divorce because it's such an emotionally charged time. Consider some of the other options that might bring stability intro your life; staying with family or friends, or even renting somewhere locally for a while might be enough to tide you over initially.

- Is it really a good idea at this time to have so much money tied up in a house? Committing to keeping the family home can feel like the best way to remain connected to normality and to our life as we knew it. But money is often an important consideration too and having large sums tied up in a house can turn out to be an expensive drain in the long-term. Deciding to sell the home and split the proceeds frees up cash, enabling our share of the money to be spent in other ways. It can be an opportunity to perhaps invest in somewhere smaller, have money with which to do other things and so ease the pressure financially.

- A family house requires regular maintenance. Yes, we may know all its idiosyncrasies, the problems with the boiler, the things that need attention, but there will be other areas that continually demand effort and expenditure. A large property has higher overheads. It demands maintenance and upkeep as well as payment of the ongoing household bills. Okay, neighbours, friends, work and children's schools may be nearby and as such are an important consideration, but there may be other, less expensive ways to support those criteria.

- Why not use the divorce as an opportunity for a fresh start? Down-sizing and beginning again in a smaller home can provide stimulus, an exciting project and an opportunity to rediscover your taste and personality. It can be a time to practice with different colours, ideas and re-establish yourself in exciting new ways. Children can put their mark on the new life and home; they can decorate their room, help with the garden and feel involved in establishing a new home.

- A house only becomes a home when time, love and attention have been lavished on it. But who's to say that you would have stayed in the marital home even if you hadn't decided to divorce? There may have come a time when you would have looked to move home and start elsewhere, perhaps retiring to a new area, down-sizing because of children moving on or re-locating because of opportunities with a work situation. It's always harder when the decision is forced on you but looking for ways to view the situation positively is an important part of the healing process.

Being flexible and weighing up all the facts can help in determining the most appropriate way to move forward after the divorce. Keeping the family home is an option, but deciding on the best option for you long-term can require a clear head and putting emotion to one side. Being confident in your decision-making process is the most positive and effective way to move on to the next phase of your life. Deciding where to live is only one way to signal a new start and a new life for yourself and those close to you.

Living Together After the Divorce

There can be a myriad of reasons why a couple choose to continue living together after their divorce. And sometimes it's possible to become good or even better friends once the marriage commitment has been dissolved.

This arrangement is often successful until one of the couple decides to embark on a new relationship. It can be difficult for the ex to accommodate a new lover in their relationship and also for a potential new lover to understand the subtleties of their partner living with their ex.

Let's look at some of the reasons why a couple may choose to still live together after they have divorced:

- Finances are often an important factor in this decision. Many couples simply cannot afford to fund two homes from the proceeds of the break-up of their family home. If the family home is spacious enough and a reasonable solution can be negotiated for bill payments and housekeeping, it may be a viable option to continue living there and establish separate living arrangements.

- Children and family are often a major consideration. Many people are loathe to be separated from their children and keeping the family home intact can sometimes be the most workable solution to the problem. Whether they be parents or childless, when both people are able to be respectful of each other this arrangement has the potential to work well enough. It can sometimes work well for their mutual families too, providing reassurance and continuity.

- Familiarity is often a major pull to stay connected. Knowing each other better than anybody else does, having shared so much of each other's lives, secrets, successes and failures counts for a lot. If a couple are not constantly arguing or there is no one else involved, living together can sometimes seem to be a reasonable solution 'for the time being'. This situation can potentially continue indefinitely.

- Practicality of domestic arrangements can sometimes provide good reasons to continue living together. The family home may be in a convenient location for work, school, family and social commitments. Working hours may complement each other with regard to childcare, animals and shopping. It may be the most practical and cost effective solution for the time being.

- Companionship can be important. Some couples continue to like each other as friends, but the intensity of their love has lessened and the chemistry has gone. The value of a good friend cannot be underestimated. Some people feel the need to divorce but are happy to continue living together in a more companionable way, free from the commitment and responsibility of a marriage.

What needs to happen to support this arrangement?

- Respect. Respecting each other's space, time and feelings are all key elements of supporting this arrangement. When two people are not married any more they need to demonstrate good manners and appreciation of each other. An important ground rule is that it's not appropriate to be manipulative or make demands on each other's time, money or emotions as an automatic right or entitlement.

- Honesty. Both have to feel comfortable about saying how they feel if the arrangement is going to work. Poor communications may well have been a contributory reason for the marriage's failure in the first place, so being honest in this new situation is crucial. As times passes there may be potential new partners appearing on the scene, so it's important to be clear, at least to oneself, about the best way to cope if this significant development does occur.

- Ground rules can help. Being clear from the outset as to basic house rules, things like finances, domestic arrangements and overnight guests, can help smooth the transition from being partners to housemates.

Unusual and unorthodox solutions can work well if both parties are prepared to be thoughtful and sensitive about each other's feelings and areas of vulnerability. Treading carefully can help to ease the new arrangements into place. After all, having been close for a time in your lives, it can potentially provide a workable solution for the next stage of your lives.

Reasons to Work From Home

Working from home has become an increasingly common choice for several reasons. Logistics, the heavy financial implications of big businesses having offices in several locations, wanting to improve the flexibility of office working hours or the desire to reduce overheads; these are all reasons why it is often deemed preferable to work from home.

Let's consider why home can be a good place to work:

- Many large organisations choose to operate from a central business headquarters, siting their management team in one location but needing their staff to work from home, from where they service their customers throughout the country. Those staff may be required to call into the central office at times for training, meetings or updates, but other times they're allowed to remain reasonably autonomous. This is often regarded as a cost effective way of running a business, eliminating the need for expensive local premises and associated staff.

- Modern technology is conducive to people working from home as it's convenient and provides easy accessibility. People can set up and work whenever they want, from anywhere they can receive a signal or internet connection. Many hotels and cafes are happy for business people to use their premises for work, networking and meetings throughout the day and there are many office spaces available to rent on an as-required basis, providing reception cover, catering and admin services, as is necessary.

- Setting up a new business can be expensive, with many decisions requiring financial investment to enable them to be implemented. Keeping overheads to a minimum can be essential to a new business's survival. Working from home, at least initially, saves on the rental of premises and other associated costs and allows for more freedom with business hours.

- Work your own hours. Unlike a shop with an 'open' or 'closed' sign on the door, no one knows what your office hours are when you work from home. Working when busy and being free to do other things like admin, cold calling and networking when the workload is quieter makes a lot of sense. A person can be on holiday and commit to spending an hour a day on the computer dealing with clients, liaising with suppliers and keeping up-to-date with their business. People with children sometimes find that they are able to work more efficiently in the evenings when there are less distractions.

- Bad weather does not concern the home worker unduly, unless clients are coming to them.

- People have to commit to come and see you. As a therapist I find that when clients make an appointment and commit to being there on time it's an important part of their commitment to getting better. And working from home provides a comfortable environment for clients to relax in, provided that it's maintained as a professional place of work.

- Family responsibilities can be taken care of much more easily by working from home. Being flexible with appointments and working hours means that chores can be done, children can be picked up from school and sick children can be looked after. Initially it may be useful to implement ground rules to ensure that work does get done. Some people like to designate certain hours or days as work time. Otherwise time can pass and the motivation to work and achieve certain goals can fade away.

Discipline and routine are crucial to effective working from home or else life can be in danger of becoming aimless and unfocussed. But running an organised and efficient business from home can enable time and energy to be used in the most viable and cost-effective ways.

Some Hints for Effective Working From Home

Many start-up businesses and sole traders work from home, at least in the early days. Managing the work environment effectively and having a clear sense of the business goals are two important areas that need to be focussed on from the outset.

One challenge in working from home is being taken seriously. I remember my mother initially saying that she thought I'd never get a 'proper job' again once I'd become a full time, home-based Counsellor and Hypnotherapist. Even though large companies find that their home-based staff regularly work harder and are more productive than their office-based staff (because they're often given specific, measurable tasks), there is still the suspicion that home workers don't take their work as seriously, that they're distracted by their household chores, are popping out to do the shopping or are watching daytime television.

Another challenge is to take ourselves seriously. Having a business plan, setting ourselves targets, goals, tasks to perform and people to meet are all signs of someone who is serious and means business. Many new start-ups find it difficult to stay focussed on their business aims and end up saying 'yes' to any offer of work that comes their way. Doing this can waste a lot of time and do damage to their reputation, by doing work that's outside their skill set.

Saying 'no' to work can be a difficult decision, but sometimes it's better to refer work to someone better suited or to form an alliance with another professional, rather than be seen as a jack of all trades. It's counter-productive to have an unclear vision of how you perceive your reputation or be vague about your goals.

One of the issues of working from home is learning when to stop working and how to switch off at the end of the day. Home workers often feel guilty at leaving work unfinished or feel that they should be doing something more. Office-based workers often have contracted work hours and then their travel time in which to mentally prepare before or draw a line after their working day. Home workers do not have that option available to them.

Here are a few hints to help home workers switch off:

- Some people find that having specific clothes that they wear for work are a help. Then at the end of the day they leave that jacket or pair of shoes 'at work'.

- If you have a defined office area, close the door or screen the desk area off. Put your books, files or computer away and symbolically close for business. Turn off the light.

- Have a separate work number that switches to answerphone out of hours.

- Leave the house and go into the garden or for a walk round the block to get some fresh air.

- Take a shower and change your clothes so that you mentally and physically freshen up for the evening

- Schedule in breaks, fun or light relief at times throughout the day, like an hour at the gym or a lunch or phone call with a friend.

It can be lonely working from home, especially as a sole trader, so finding ways to introduce business support can make a difference to stress levels, motivation and satisfaction:

- Find an energetic networking group. Some meet online, others in person, and offer the opportunity to meet like-minded professionals to share tips, advice and receive support.

- Bodies are available, some through the Government, which provide funding, coaching, training courses and support to start-ups and new businesses. Forms need to be filled in and certain criteria met, but they can be an effective way of getting your business off the ground.

- Keep your admin and books up-to-date. Set aside time to deal with paperwork and accounts on a regular basis. This avoids your home becoming deluged with piles of stressful outstanding invoices, orders and mail and removes the annual crisis of submitting your accounts on time. It also gives you control over your business, enabling you to see at a glance where you are in terms of pricing, billing, being paid and profit margins.

- Review your business plan regularly, whilst being receptive to new ideas and opportunities. Discuss your business goals regularly with your adviser or accountant and identify where your strengths lie.

- Stay in touch with people in your profession, either through your association or at conferences. It's important to know the latest news, developments and initiatives that are happening in your field and it can be lonely working on your own, so stay connected.

Working from home can offer the best or the worst of solutions and finding ways to manage the negative side of it can provide you with a suitable balance to your life, where you can ultimately work as much or as little as you choose.

Tips for Remaining in Your Own Home in Later Life

For many of us our home is the embodiment of who we are. It houses our lives, our accumulated possessions and memories, the different tastes and inspirations that have influenced us over the years, as well as the many stories and experiences that we have lived through whilst residing there.

The thought of leaving to live somewhere else is often stressful. It can be upsetting to have to accept that we are becoming older and less capable and in control as we'd like to be. Moving somewhere smaller can be viewed as a step to redress the balance, a gesture to reclaim some of our independence and autonomy by having less responsibility to worry about.

There can be several valid considerations about moving home; should we move somewhere smaller so that it's less expensive and easier to manage or should we look to release some capital so that we can spend the money elsewhere? Do we move from a house to an apartment? What are the implications, especially if we now live alone?

There's often a certain logic to down-sizing, but for many people the words 'not just yet' ring out loud. So instead, let's look at some ways that remaining in your own home can be feasible.

- Get help. Some chores can become increasingly arduous as we get older. Would it be possible to get help with heavy cleaning, gardening and shopping? Even if someone were to help only occasionally it could support you in remaining in your home and be one less burden to consider.

- Meals can be regularly delivered as required. This can ensure that you have at least one cooked meal a day. The service can be arranged through your doctor or social services or through a private supplier and, like having a home help, it means that there will be someone calling on you too.

- Buy a computer. Computers have made life easier for many people. Shopping can be done online and then delivered to your door. Everything you could want from food, books, clothes and presents can all be bought online and then promptly delivered, often the next day. Email, skype and social networking sites provide easy contact with friends and family, wherever they may be, and offer the potential to connect with new friends and have interesting company at your convenience.

- Consider a pet. A pet can be a wonderful source of love, attention and companionship and they make a house feel like a home. Many hospitals have discovered the therapeutic value of having a friendly dog come to visit. Stroking, grooming and watching their antics are all calming activities. But a pet is also a serious responsibility, especially as we get older.

A dog needs to be walked, whatever the weather. But that can be good, as many people make new friends whilst out walking their dog. Pets are demanding though and need attention, feeding and sometimes medical care. It's wonderful to have a bird or an animal greet you first thing in the morning or when you arrive home, but they are an expense, a commitment and have to be considered whenever you make plans to go away for any length of time.

- Be vigilant about keeping fit and healthy. Remaining in your own home requires you to feel confident about your ability to cope. Pay attention to aches or pains and ensure that any symptoms are treated speedily. Be aware of any changes in your mood. For some people the prospect of becoming older can be difficult to come to terms with. Counselling and hypnotherapy are positive ways to support your confidence, attitude and help with any stress or anxiety-related symptoms like poor sleeping patterns or low mood and depression.

- Try to exercise regularly. Even if it's only a walk to the local shop, ensure that you undertake regular exercise. There are some good workouts that can be done sitting down, so exercise and keeping fit is possible at any level. Similarly mental activity is important. Puzzles, crosswords and bridge are all ways to keep your mind alert and exercised.

- Think about sharing your home. Might it be a viable option to convert part of your family home into a granny flat for you, with your family living next door in the main part of the house? This decision can provide the best of both worlds; independence for you whilst still remaining in your own home, with family companionship and support close by. For other families selling their individual homes and buying a larger one to share jointly is a variation on this option.

Any potential change to your circumstances requires a variety of options to be considered and compromises to be made. By being aware of the many different possibilities you improve your chances of finding the most beneficial outcome at the time.

CHAPTER SEVEN

Stress and Health

The Importance of Balance in Life as a Way to Manage Stress

Balance is something that is useful to apply to many different areas of life. It can help us moderate our mannerisms, desires, temperament and lifestyle and can introduce a healthier outlook into our lives. Many people feel that when they are balanced they are able to look at life from a calmer, less stressed perspective. They can often understand situations with a more even viewpoint.

Let's look at areas where it's good to find balance:

- **Food** is an important pleasure in many people's lives and indeed, many social activities include nibbles, treats, dinner and desserts. An excess of food can cause health and weight-related issues. Some people think about food constantly. People on slimming diets often think about what they have already eaten and what they are going to eat next. Planning meals can become almost an obsession. They will sometimes eat and then be filled with loathing as they analyse their calorie intake. Low confidence levels are often an important factor with food and comfort eating. Often counselling can help people understand and come to terms with their relationship with food.

Other people eat and then forget about food. They may well have enjoyed their meal, but it is simply one small part of life. They regard it as fuel and only stop to refuel when they are almost on empty. Balance is about enjoying eating, allowing it to be a pleasurable experience at certain times of the day. Taking time to stop and enjoy a meal can provide a valuable break, maybe an opportunity to chat and mix with others, to discuss the day and reconnect with family and friends. It can be a time to take in valuable nutrition, de-stress, unwind and enjoy some pleasant company.

- **Drink** features in many social situations, but balance is an important aspect of alcohol consumption. Being able to enjoy a good quality wine or a glass of beer, but also being able to take it or leave it is a useful approach to adopt with alcohol. All too often people link alcohol with stress and de-stressing. Winding down with an alcoholic drink at the end of a stressful day can be very relaxing but it can become a habit, where the volume gradually increases. An occasional glass can escalate into regularly drinking a lot every day.

- **Exercise** links well with health care. It helps us manage weight, supports body health, staves off illness and infection and is a good way to keep one's mood elevated through stimulating endorphins as we de-stress. Exercise can also be a good way of connecting with other people. Shared walks, games and sports are a good way to enjoy company whilst gaining some valuable health benefits. Balance in exercise is about appreciating the importance of committing to some healthy exercise, making it an important part of life and health. It is about taking the time to participate in some form of exercise maybe three times a week, but not becoming obsessive about it.

- **Possessions.** Gaining success is often demonstrated through the acquisition of wealth and possessions. But an excess of affluence can become counter-productive and de-motivational. It can bring with it apathy, indifference and a sense of entitlement. People who use financial success as a motivator often find that when they reach that level of success, money alone is not enough. Many people find that money does not bring satisfaction. Other factors are important, like achievement, fulfilment, being useful. It's the journey to success that motivates, with all its challenges and effort.

Many people reach a time in their lives or a level of financial security where they choose to down-size and do something that brings a different sort of quality of life. They need to have enough money to live on, but weigh that up against the satisfaction of how they decide to spend their days. Some people choose to introduce different challenges into their life; open a new business, do charity work, re-train in a new skill or set an exciting target. Conversely, people who feel that they have no real goals, that everything is a struggle, that they are merely surviving, can become stressed and de-motivated as they feel unfulfilled with their lives.

- **Work** is the way that many people define themselves. If you ask a person to talk about themselves they will often start by telling you what they do for a living. We spend most of our waking hours at work or thinking about it when we are not there. We may fret over concerns about future prospects and success. But balance also includes taking time off, having appropriate breaks, stopping for meals, having holidays and then returning to work with a more positive and recharged attitude. Work provides occupation and usefulness for people, but should also allow time for other interests too.

Wake Up Well and Start Your Day Feeling Great

How we awaken in the morning can impact on the rest of the day. If we wake up feeling jaded, in need of more sleep or stressed and overwhelmed at the prospect of the coming day we may need to reflect on our habits and the way we manage our lives. Let's look at some ways to better support yourself and your quality of life.

- **Commit to getting more sleep**. Many people simply don't get enough sleep. They work longer and longer hours, sometimes right through until bedtime when they fall into bed, exhausted and hoping to drift off into a deep, refreshing night-long sleep. It's hardly surprising that their minds are racing or that they have restless sleep and disturbing dreams.

  Instead, try to treat sleep as an important part of your commitment to good health and plan to sleep well. Take some positive steps to take control of your life and notice how your quality of sleep improves and how much more positive you feel when you awaken in the morning.

- **Plan for the coming day** by using lists so that when you wake you feel prepared, clear-headed and ready for the day ahead. Sometimes it's worth taking thirty minutes on a Sunday evening to plan an overview of the coming week so that you can focus and be more in control of your time. Granted, new, unexpected things have a habit of cropping up, but if you are clear about your major commitments it gives you more flexibility and the ability to manoeuvre whenever necessary.

- **Prepare the night before** for a positive start to each day. Put your clothes out and make your packed lunch so that it's ready to go. Set your radio alarm to a pleasant station, one that's not too jarring as you wake up. Early morning light can be an issue for some people. It's possible to buy bedside lamps that gradually introduce you to the light as they slowly become brighter. Then get up to an energising shower using lively citrus fragrances so that you wake up well, with a spring in your step.

- Some people like to **start the day with exercise**, but if you're not one of those people who relish a bike ride to the office or an early morning visit to the gym, it's still possible to enjoy a fifteen/twenty-minute stretch routine or a little early morning yoga. Many people enjoy gentle exercise as a positive way to start the day, allowing them to feel calmer, more relaxed and grounded before they leave their home. Spending a little time outside in the fresh air can be a valuable way to incorporate meditation or deep breathing as well as introducing a little 'me time' into a busy day.

- **Good food and nutrition** is an important way to wake up well, with a healthy start, but not everyone likes to take breakfast. Some people prefer to grab a coffee on the way to the office. A healthier, more beneficial way to introduce the day is to get up a few minutes earlier and allow time to make yourself a nutritious juice, full of fresh fruit and vegetables. You can drink it as you get ready, knowing that you're giving your body a positive start, as you incorporate several of your 'five a day' before you even leave your home.

How you wake up can spread ripples throughout your life. It influences how you interact with others and that in turn affects their mood and the quality of their day. So it's important to do your best to ensure that you wake up well and start your day as you mean to go on, feeling as great as possible.

Could Your Symptoms be Stress Related?

Many people don't appreciate the impact that stress is having upon them, on their bodies, health and wellbeing. They may be aware that they're busy, have too much to do each day, but they accept it as a normal part of being a parent, having a career, running a business. They may not have time to consider what's happening to their bodies; it's enough just to get through each day.

If we were to walk across the road at a leisurely pace and a car came hurtling towards us we would automatically enter the self-preservation fight or flight mode. In the face of immediate, life-threatening danger we have to quickly determine whether it's best to stay and fight or kick up our heels and run away. Once we've reached the other side of the road we'll probably need a minute to calm down and recover from feeling shaky. We may experience jelly legs, a pounding heart, dizziness, a shortness of breath, churning stomach and/or dry mouth, but we would understand why we felt that way.

Think about how many of those symptoms may be with you on a regular basis, as a matter of course. How many of us live in a constant stressed state, juggling too many balls in the air, hardly able to breathe? Often the language we use is an indicator of what's going on in our bodies. We may internalize the pressures but our choice of words often reveals what's going on within.

- **'It's doing my head in'** is a phrase many people use to refer to feeling overwhelmed, having too many demands on them, on their time and goodwill. This may result in headaches, frustration, irritability, loss of sense of humour and reduced libido as pressures continue in their lives. Some people try to cope with excessive demands by missing meals, drinking coffee to stay awake, working till the last-minute before collapsing into bed, exhausted but mind racing at what still needs to be done or could have been done better.

  If this sounds like you some relief may come from learning to say 'no' and starting to communicate your feelings appropriately to others. Take control and ask for help, delegate or explain what's going on and enable others to become aware of the pressures you're dealing with.

- **'I'm gutted/sick to my stomach'**. Irritable bowel syndrome and other gut-related issues are often exacerbated by stress and pressure. Learning to relax, take breaks, follow a healthy diet can all benefit gut-related symptoms. Some people learn to recognise their personal amber lights, their individual warning signs that stress levels are rising to an unacceptable level. For some people it may be that their stomach goes 'off' and they start having digestive problems. Tune-in to your body and learn to recognise your personal warning signs. Then you can begin to intercept them earlier, before things become too much of a problem.

- **'It really gets under my skin'.** These words can be accompanied by itchy, irritated skin, rashes or flare ups of old skin conditions. Look at what's causing irritation in your life, things that you are struggling to say or deal effectively with. Suppressed feelings can cause stress to come out in this way.

- **'I can't see straight'.** Blurred vision, spots before the eyes and headaches can occur through stress. Feeling overloaded with choices or tasks can impact on your ability to see and prioritize the most appropriate next step. You may find that you become reactive, constantly dropping what you're working on in order to begin the next task or piece of work, so leaving older tasks unfinished. Frustration, irritation, feeling overwhelmed can result, often exacerbated when irate customers, friends and family demand to know what's going on. Communicating with others, installing systems and processes, becoming effective at note-taking and using lists can all help in managing a busy life.

- **'I can't think straight'.** Stress can impact so much on their thinking that some people may begin to feel they're losing their mind. They may find themselves constantly checking things as their memory becomes hazy, their concentration impaired. They may worry that these symptoms indicate they're suffering from early stages of Dementia or Alzheimer's Disease, which in turn increases the stress and pressure that they're experiencing. Techniques to reduce stress levels can bring significant benefits; being committed to regular quality sleep, a healthy diet and exercise regime, enlisting the support of family, friends and colleagues if applicable, can all help to minimise stress and improve the quality of life.

Don't forget though, that physical symptoms can be a warning that something is amiss with your body. Be sure to have a check-up with your doctor if you have concerns about symptoms, especially if they persist. It's important to take responsibility for your health.

Let's Look at Pain and How It's Affected by Stress.

Pain is our body's way of telling us that something is wrong. Some people may experience short-term pain, after an accident, an operation or an injury. Other people may have ongoing pain as the result of a chronic or acute condition. Then there are different levels of pain; continuous or intermittent, intense or less severe.

There are several factors to consider with pain and it's important to our ultimate relief and comfort to consider these.

- With any pain the first step is to get checked by a doctor. He or she will usually run a battery of tests, to see what's going on and provide guidance, advice and treatment if required. These days there are many successful ways to manage pain but finding the appropriate balance of treatment can take a little time and experimentation.

- Often there is a psychological component to pain, which needs consideration. Think of how we talk when we are hurt, distressed or feeling low. Much of our language has a physical reference to it. We talk about being broken-hearted, gutted, irritated and our bodies can be affected by those words.

- Stress is often an important factor. Stress causes more cortisol to be generated as a response to perceived danger and emergency situations, which can heighten the body's experience of pain. Think of how you tense and hold yourself rigid if you anticipate being hurt by something.

- There are hundreds of symptoms of stress and many include physical upset and pain. Palpitations, bodily discomfort and insomnia can all be linked to stress. Pain can be factor as a result of these symptoms. When a person is stressed they become more aware of how their body feels. Every twinge, ache or sensation can become magnified and focussed on. This can serve to heighten any pain and discomfort.

- Physical problems can be exacerbated by pain. We hold ourselves differently in order to avoid hurting ourselves more when we are in pain. This can lead to us putting extra strain on other parts of our body and experiencing referred pain as a consequence. By walking differently, holding ourselves in an awkward or unusual position our body goes out of alignment and can become increasingly hurt, strained or damaged. Also the by-product of ongoing, sustained pain can be stress, low mood, weariness and feeling out of sorts.

Things You Can Do to Help You Manage Pain:

- Manage stress better. Notice your personal signals that occur when you start to feel distressed and overwhelmed. Some people get headaches, others lose their sense of humour or sleeping patterns may become affected. We all have our warning indicators that begin when we feel stressed and unhappy. Learn to recognise them. That way you can start to treat yourself better and intercept the pain. Take a break, have a walk in the park, do something that provides an interlude to help manage the stress effectively and helps you to relax and enjoy better health.

- Commit to taking better care of yourself at all times. Some people with ongoing health-related conditions find that when they feel a little better they try to over-compensate for all the good times and fun that they've missed. Then they become over-tired, end up in pain, feeling unwell again. It's important to set good habits in place. Regular rest, a healthy diet and a good balance to life are all important ways of looking after yourself.

- Learn self-hypnosis. This is a powerful technique to support better pain management. Learn to scale pain and turn it down a little, or introduce techniques for visualising healing and feeling stronger. These can help with the associated attitude and confidence aspects of your condition. Then you can feel more in control, as you manage your health and your quality of life more effectively.

Pain is often a signal that something is wrong. Respect that signal, listen to its message but then learn to manage and deal with it as healthfully and positively as possible. The thing about pain is, whenever possible, not to let it impact too much upon your life.

The Power of the Placebo

Have you noticed how much interest there is of late in the power of the placebo? Many people are awakening to the fact that the mind has amazing abilities, above and beyond what's deemed to be logical, rational or readily explained. Many of us already know from personal experience, without the benefit of scientific research, that when we focus our minds, believe something is possible we significantly improve our chances of success.

Placebos buy into our belief system and the literal way we're able to interpret information. So, as previously discussed, if we say 'I'm gutted', 'sick to my stomach', 'he's a pain in the neck' or 'she's really got under my skin' regularly and with conviction it's no surprise if we start to experience a negative physical effect that reflects those words. Similarly, when we visualise, repeat affirmations or focus our minds on a positive outcome we invest in our greater chances of success.

It is widely accepted that our minds, combined with any stress we may be experiencing are a major factor of physical symptoms, of aches, pains and complaints. Headaches, Irritable Bowel Syndrome, sleeping problems, dizziness, depleted immune system are just some of the physical symptoms exacerbated by sustained mental stress. When we address those factors, manage how we think, feel and speak we become better able to function well; we become healthier and live a better quality of life. Simply by smiling, looking upwards and standing straighter we begin to introduce a healthier, more positive mind-set.

So it follows that if a medical person, a trusted doctor says 'take this, it will make you feel better' chances are the recipient will believe him or her and invest their hopes for recovery in that treatment. When we trust someone, want to believe what they say, need to have faith in a positive outcome we invest as fully as we're able. Interestingly, people have even reported side effects when coming off placebos. They were so committed to their medication that when the time came to end the treatment they experienced withdrawal symptoms.

A placebo may typically be a sugar pill, something with no active ingredients that can readily be accepted as authentic medicine and taken with confidence by the patient. It can be a treatment, procedure or process. Research suggests that placebos provide significant benefits to the recipients. Clinical trials running blind or even double-blind tests report that placebos regularly provide positive results in well over half their patients. They show that when the mind believes something strongly enough that belief is able to bring about amazing results.

Historically there have been many examples of the power of the placebo. Large scale tragedies, war zones, catastrophes, emergency situations where medication has been in short supply have on occasion required medical teams to rely on placebos to treat their patients, either when resorting to using ineffective medicine and/or telling patients that they're going to be fine. These results have been surprisingly positive.

Until relatively recently it was felt that benefits were achieved through purely psychological means. However research into the management of pain using placebos has shown that biological, physical changes also occur in the body. Dopamine production has been shown to increase with the introduction of a placebo. This is the brain chemical associated with reward and pleasure. It introduces a feel good sensation into the body, helping to minimise the experience of pain.

It is strongly suggested that if we are told by someone we trust, someone we know and like or by a professional in whom we have confidence, that if we proceed with a particular medicine, undergo a treatment or follow a procedure it will benefit us, cure us or alleviate our suffering there is a greater likelihood of us undertaking it successfully.

Patients who have previous successful experience of a treatment regime will already have confidence in its ability to help and be more likely to be mentally receptive to it. They will be conditioned to expect a positive result from repeating the process. Positive expectations are an important factor in the successful use of placebos.

The mind has incredible power. Self-help books on the power of affirmations, books that teach the ability to attract good results, which support our ability to influence our success are best sellers. Positive beliefs enable us to engage more fully, override negative thought patterns and harness our power for good. When we believe in something we are able to fully focus on it, often to the exclusion of any other possibility. As such we lift our spirits, raise our expectations, introduce a lighter, happier perspective and, consequently, feel more hopeful.

As an aside, this is why there is often less success in patients with Alzheimer's Disease. Using placebos or indeed any medication for pain relief in these patients is less effective because they often have limited expectations; they are more forgetful, less able to imagine or entertain the possibility of feeling better. Reduced capacity for imagination, belief or being able to see the bigger picture often limits the potential for success in these patients.

Stress and its Impact on Sleep

Stress is an increasing factor of daily life. Worries about job security, finances, crime levels and the pressures of modern life are becoming more and more prevalent. Some stress is fine - it keeps us on our toes and can often push us into achieving more than we initially thought we could or would.

However, living in a constant stressful state is a damaging way to live. The impact of living with sustained stress can filter through and impact in many areas - health, relationships, attitude and behaviour. Instead of having a 'green for go' traffic light, where everything is going well, the 'amber warning light', or even the 'red stop light', starts to flash and symptoms begin to appear that affect our health and well-being.

There are reportedly 360 symptoms of stress and anxiety; from headaches, blurred vision, insomnia, miscellaneous aches and pains and poor concentration. Personal relationships can suffer because of reduced levels of patience, good humour and increased irritability. Some people may find that they turn increasingly to alcohol, junk food, drugs and caffeine hits to find comfort, support and help.

Sleeping patterns are often disrupted as a consequence, so that getting to sleep, insomnia or fitful sleep becomes a problem. This can cause real problems because sleep is an important way of allowing the body to heal, recuperate and detoxify, whilst allowing the mind to calm and soothe itself. Often the phrase 'sleep on it' is used to good effect, by allowing the conscious mind to take time out so that the unconscious mind can explore alternative options and perspectives on matters of concern.

Tired and in Need of a Good Night's Sleep?

Modern life is stressful, with many of us regularly working from morning till night, cramming every second full of activity. Family and work responsibilities, the expectations of friends or the chance of grabbing a few minutes of respite for ourselves can all mean that every minute of the day is filled with meaningful activity. It's no wonder that when we fall into bed at night we're exhausted, with mind racing, desperate for a good night's sleep.

Often though we may be restless, find it difficult to drift off to sleep or awaken during the night, wide awake and unable to go back to sleep after only a few fitful hours. 90% of adults say that they don't get enough sleep and when they do sleep, find that it's not restful or restorative. Let's look at how even those busy people can negotiate with their lives and find ways to support a deep, refreshing good night's sleep.

- **Learning to prioritize** is a useful skill in a busy life. Poor sleep often occurs when we work long hours or have too much on our minds. Prioritising introduces some discipline and order, helps us to make the best use of our time. Lists can be an effective way of noting everything that needs to be done, then going through the list and clarifying the degree of urgency of each individual item.

- **Recognise your personal warning signs** of becoming stressed and over tired. I referred to those 'amber lights' earlier as being the time when you start to notice your mood changing and irritability, loss of sense of humour, poor concentration or feeling unwell begins to occur. As you start to recognise when negative changes in your demeanour begin to appear you can schedule in effective ways to take better care of yourself, take time out and reduce the impact of stress overload.

- **Establish balance in your life.** Poor sleep can occur when you're tired mentally but not physically, or vice versa. If you have work that requires significant mental effort, where you perhaps spend a lot of time indoors, try to ensure you have breaks where you engage in physical activity and spend time outdoors in nature. Use free time for gardening, walking along a beach, going for a run in the countryside or playing sport with others if possible. If you have a physically taxing job try to have regular mental exertion like reading, puzzles, interesting conversations that require you to think and exercise your mental abilities.

- **Can you find a way to schedule a nap at lunchtime?** Many big businesses now provide the opportunity for staff to take sleep breaks when they're tired. Some even provide sleeping pods. They appreciate the value of having employees who are rested, clear-headed, motivated and able to think straight. Managing your tiredness helps you to feel more balanced throughout the day and less exhausted as the day draws to a close. Even if you're only occasionally able to park your car and rest or sit in the park for a few minutes, it's important to find time whenever you can for a break.

- **Commit time to winding down** for a couple of hours before bed. Turn off your technology, avoid stressful conversations, horror films and heavy meals late at night. Go for a walk, practice yoga, try hypnotherapy or have a lovely bath to wash away the day's stresses and concerns; use those lovely scented candles you've been saving for a special occasion.

- **Make your bedroom a haven** for sleep, relaxation and personal time. Screen off any work-related area and avoid having your mobile phone or TV too close to the bed. Keep your bedroom free from clutter. Choose lovely, soothing colours, textures and fragrances and ensure it's a pleasant, well-ventilated, relaxing room.

- **Your bed is important**. It's worth spending money on a comfortable bed, pillows and bedding. You spend a reasonable amount of time in bed so consider the money an investment in yourself and your health.

- **Little touches can make a difference** to your quality of sleep. Add lavender to the final rinse cycle of your sheets. Resist the temptation to take food, work or books to bed. Listen to relaxing music. Allow your mind to calm and become still, ready for sleep. Then you'll find the overall quality of your sleep and consequently your life improves.

Do You Struggle with Sunday Night Insomnia?

A 2015 report revealed that Sunday night insomnia is an issue for as many as one in four of us. Those afflicted may go to bed early, feel tired and are keen to go off to sleep. Instead they lie awake tossing and turning or they drift off to sleep only to awaken in the early hours feeling tired and unrefreshed. What is it about weekends and especially Sunday nights that can cause such a level of sleep disturbance?

For many people weekends are about quality time, special time to be spent with family and friends, doing meaningful things with the important people in their lives. But chores need to be fitted in too and this can result in every second being accounted for, with little space for relaxation and chilling out.

Then there are those people who prefer not to have plans at the weekend. They want to be spontaneous and see how things pan out, but they can end up doing nothing or very little. This can result in them feeling cheated, that they've wasted their weekend and as such they can feel frustrated at the amount of time they've frittered away.

Often 'friends' will have posted pictures and updates on social media about the scintillating weekend they've had partying with friends, having a simply fabulous time in all the local bars and hot spots. This can serve to highlight one's own shortcomings in the fun department, even though we know only too well that social media is specifically tailored to publicise what a great time has been had, to post pictures of lots of fun and laughter.

Sunday night is also the time when many people start to reflect on the coming week at work. They may be due to receive feedback on a crucial piece of work they've delivered or have a busy time ahead with important meetings. Perhaps there's a large volume of outstanding work to clear, staff shortages to accommodate. There may be ongoing tension with a colleague or job security may be an issue. Added into the mix is the stress of the daily commute with traffic, road conditions and other commuters to navigate, plus any personal or domestic concerns.

All these factors can influence our ability to sleep well on a Sunday night. And let's not forget that our habits are often very different at weekends. I've worked with clients who've experienced dreadful headaches at weekends only to be incredulous when they calculate how much coffee they drink during their working week compared to a much lesser amount at weekends - the caffeine withdrawal causes their weekend headaches!

Let's look at ways to help you sleep better on a Sunday night:

- **Deal with any worries** as best you can. Write down outstanding items on a list and question each item in turn. Ask 'can I do anything more about it', 'have I done as much as I can?'. Deal with what you're able to and then decide to put the worry list away in a drawer until the situation moves or changes. This can be a useful discipline to employ, providing reassurance that you won't forget anything serious or important; it's written down, so you don't need to constantly turn it over in your head.

- **Share how you're feeling**. Discuss matters with close family or friends and listen to their issues in return. It can be heartening to discover that you're not alone in your concerns and you may find that you end up sharing advice and solutions, helping each other with mutual support.

- **Plan your weekends ahead.** Rather than leave things to chance or alternatively have each minute choreographed why not take time to sensibly plan ahead, incorporating time for chores, catching up with friends as well as a little personal time. Maybe double up some arrangements and go for a walk, followed by Sunday lunch with a group of friends. That way you combine fresh air, exercise and time socialising with the special people in your life.

- It can be useful to **set aside thirty minutes on a Sunday night** to plan an overview of the coming week. Then when new or unexpected issues arise you have a better sense of how you can accommodate them. You're able to feel less stressed and more in control.

- **Don't be afraid to say 'no'.** Sometimes declining invitations can be a positive commitment to yourself and to your quality of life. Instead of going to yet another party or meal with friends why not have a relaxing night at home with your special someone over a take-away supper and a little TV. It can be a lovely, less tiring way to spend an evening. Soften the refusal by offering an alternative date for meeting up with those friends.

A few simple actions can relieve the pressure, so enabling you to feel more relaxed and less stressed about the coming week at work; some pointers to help you sleep better on a Sunday night!

Can Dreams Solve Emotional Problems?

Dreams are the time when our conscious minds are suspended from being engaged and alert, so allowing our unconscious minds to run free and explore different options and solutions to any problems we may be encountering in our day to day lives. Anything is possible in a dream. That's why people often experience dreams of a curious mixture of fantasy and reality. The unconscious mind can utilise symbolism and metaphors to explore any possibilities that it wishes.

In real life we cannot fly unaided or fight a dragon, but these things are possible in our dreams, so giving us power, strength and unlimited resources to deal with situations that in real life we need assistance with. We're able to run with our emotions and responses, deal with negative feelings and so allow ourselves to feel better as a result.

Understanding our dreams provides us with important information. Emotional problems can have deep rooted origins. They are often influenced by how we are treated in our everyday life. Becoming more assertive and less compliant or needy can often turn a relationship around and enable it to be more evenly balanced.

Negative patterns may go back to our earlier life, sometimes to childhood. Appreciating the longstanding influence of things we've experienced and the consequences of witnessing other people's relationships and interactions can be a very cathartic experience.

Exploring and dealing with these insights in our dreams is a very effective way of healing old unwanted patterns of behaviour. The symbolism can be fascinating to interpret. We may utilise things from everyday life, or we may use situations and people from the world of celebrity or characters from films and literature to act out our issues.

Feelings and relationships in dreams are often represented by water. Everything is important. The colour is relevant, light or dark can reflect the mood of the situation. Is the water deep or shallow, and how does that feel; okay or scary? Is the surface smooth or choppy? All these factors have their part to play in the unfolding story of the dream. How we feel as the story evolves is the key to understanding our dream's symbolism and message.

Oftentimes the dreamer is represented by a building or house. Previously undiscovered rooms can mean that we are opening ourselves up to new undiscovered potential. We are letting parts of ourselves, previously closed off, become available again. Shabby or untouched rooms can mean that we have left parts of ourselves neglected or under-developed for some time.

Emotional aspects of the building are often about trusting someone or concern at becoming vulnerable in a new relationship. Also there may well be issues around having to make an effort to smarten ourselves up to accommodate a new relationship. 'Will I be good enough?' may be an issue.

Familiar people in dreams may feature in order to address their impact on our lives, deal with associated issues or find a solution to a troubling aspect of the dreamer's life. Famous people in dreams often represent a characteristic or trait that they are identified with. Those characteristics can be either good or bad, but are able to be utilised to work through the situation and explore options to resolve matters.

Using dreams to address, heal and resolve our emotional issues offers an opportunity to import additional skills and resources. These innate skills have often lain dormant until it becomes necessary for the dreamer to use them to address problem areas. Dreaming can help us to solve our emotional problems by using metaphors or symbols. They enable us to recognise, understand, heal, let go, resolve matters and then adjust psychologically. Understanding our dreams enables us to de-stress and begin letting go of tensions that have been disturbing our daily lives, so bringing about a healthier way of coping and a more positive mind-set.

Why Wait to Lose Weight?

Weight can be a difficult issue. Many people know what the 'good' healthy foods are, what they should be eating in order to maintain a healthy weight, but putting that knowledge into practice is not so easy. Food has so many associations. As well as nutrition it can also embody treats, comfort, affluence, quality of life and sociability. Whilst we have to eat sensibly to live and be healthy it can be hard to sustain changes to our diet when we have got into bad habits.

Let's look at some ways for you to introduce better lifestyle choices with a view to losing weight:

- Hypnotherapy can be a great option when you need to focus your mind on your weight loss goal. It enables your mind to remove the association with edible treats as a way of managing stress and let go of the unhealthy associations with certain foods that may have been a part of your previous conditioning. You can then really begin to mentally visualise and experience the image of how you want to look and feel, begin to really connect with your target size and shape.

  By utilising the power of the mind you can commit to overcoming any underlying issues with food and eating. Often there are emotional triggers to eating. You may find that you eat for comfort or as a way to alleviate stress, or at times when you are upset and in need of a tasty reward. Food can even be used as a way to discourage unwanted attention through eating so much that you lose your appealing figure. Hypnotherapy can help to improve your confidence so that you treat yourself in a more appropriate way.

- Children often expect sweets, cakes, biscuits, crisps, or snacks as a reward for good behaviour or when they return home from school or after playing out. All too often though I hear that it's the Mums who are the ones who most frequently raid the biscuit jar or eat the sweets and chocolate. If you feel that your children must have these treats why not instead give them money so that they can buy whatever they want, rather than you keeping a tempting stock in the house!

- Water is important. Many people think that they are hungry when in reality they are thirsty. Drinking still water thirty minutes before a meal and keeping regularly hydrated throughout the day can help you feel less in need of snacks throughout the day and full sooner. Still water is better than the fizzy kind.

- Don't eat because the clock says it's a meal time or because there's a gap in your schedule during which you feel you'd better eat just in case there's no time later on. Wait until you're hungry to eat. Keep healthy snacks like washed fruit and nuts handy for snacks. Apples, bananas, grapes, nuts are a great alternative to sugary snacks.

- Sleep properly. Being over-tired and stressed can hijack your metabolic rate and interfere with weight loss. It can be hard to know if you're hungry when you're tired or stressed and it can be tempting to resort to sugar and caffeine to artificially boost your energy levels in order to get through each day.

- Ready meals, processed food and take-aways can seem like a quick, easy solution at the end of a busy day or week, but are unhealthy as a regular option. Try cooking ahead, doing a major batch preparation and putting home-cooked meals in the freezer. That way there's something healthy available and ready to eat for dinner each night when you come home. Or salads can often be made quite quickly.

- While the evening meal is cooking why not get your partner or family to go for a walk. It can be a lovely opportunity to spend thirty minutes together before homework, television or the evening proper starts. At weekends it can be fun to organise games like football, cricket, rounders, so that everyone can spend time together whilst exercising. Family walks and bike rides, hunting for shells on the beach, bird watching in the woods, are all fun ways of getting outdoors, reconnecting with your family and friends, exercising and leading less sedentary lives.

- Change to healthier options. Wholegrain or wholemeal bread is more satisfying nutritionally than white bread; parsnips and sweet potatoes are a healthy alternative to potatoes. Choose water rather than fizzy drinks. Organic food contains less chemicals and additives than other foods. Being more aware of what you're buying and paying a little more attention to your choices supports better health and improves your chances of successful weight loss and introducing better long-term eating habits.

Introducing new routines can take time and effort initially. Planning ahead requires some organisation until it becomes second nature, but it's worth taking better care of your health, your diet and your weight levels. That way you function better and improve your quality of life.

Tasty Treats - No Calories in Sight!

Granted, there are times when we really need a treat. We may feel unhappy, overtired, or maybe we are maybe having problems with our partner, work or children. There may be times when we feel that we deserve something nice as a reward. These are the occasions when we feel compelled to indulge ourselves, have something rather nice to help us get through the situation, cosset ourselves a little, feel good about ourselves or help to relieve the stress. These are typically our vulnerable times.

Often sugary treats are the ones that we reach for. Biscuits, cakes, chocolates and maybe alcohol soothe us into a calmer place mentally. But do they? How often after we have indulged do we berate ourselves for having been weak, for eating more than we needed, for consuming that packet of biscuits, bar of chocolate or drinking too much wine!

Let's look at some wonderful treats that can help us feel good, satisfied and yet contain not a single calorie.

- A vase of fresh flowers introduces colour and fragrance, as well as looking beautiful wherever you display them. Put them somewhere different, like your bedroom or the bathroom, so that when you see them you smile at having bought something as a treat just for you.

- Freshly laundered sheets on your bed, maybe with a hint of essential oils in the final rinse cycle are a lovely treat at the end of a busy, stressful day. They help you sleep better and make bedtime a more relaxing time. Turn your bedroom into a comfortable haven.

- Take the afternoon off. Put yourself in your diary and go for a walk in the park on your own. Stop and enjoy the peace and quiet, the opportunity to go wherever you like. Maybe feed the ducks or visit the petting zoo. Have a quiet, peaceful afternoon.

- Listen to music, either at home or in your car. Find somewhere you can close the door, relax and listen to your favourite tracks.

- Book a massage, facial or manicure. Spending a little time and money on a treatment for yourself can make you feel indulgent, more confident and ready to enjoy the fact that you are investing in yourself and your own well-being. A massage is a great way to de-stress.

- Locate your photograph albums and spend a nostalgic hour or two being reminiscent about old times. Or maybe amuse yourself by reading your old diaries or some long-forgotten letters. Having a laugh, cry or rueful smile about the past can be a lovely way to spend a little time.

- Get up early and watch the sun rise. Maybe take a walk or a jog in the early hours when no one else is around.

- Introduce different colours into your home. Bright cushions, prints and ornaments can make an enormous improvement and be done without too much expense. They add a personal touch and can make your home feel fresh and inviting.

- Candle light is lovely in the evening. It can create a relaxing, self-indulgent atmosphere, even when you're on your own. A real treat!

- Take the time to sit and read a book, poetry or a magazine. Or catch up on those films that you've recorded but never found the time to watch.

- Spend time in the garden. Maybe grow plants or your own vegetables. A little effort can bring rewards by way of colour, fresh produce, and somewhere to sit on a pleasant afternoon.

- Organise a walk for friends or visit the various entertainment options that are available. Museums, libraries and art galleries often have free exhibitions and some places provide free concerts.

- Take a bath and use a hair or relaxing facial treatment at the same time. You could add scented candles and soothing music and make it really special.

- Go to bed for half an hour. A nap can really lift your spirits and revitalise you for the rest of the day.

- Phone a friend. Make a drink and allow the time for a real chat, just like you would if you were together.

These are just a few of my ideas that introduce you to a positive way to have time and thought for yourself. By bringing some of these ideas into your life you can feel rewarded, special and have no guilt about your behaviour afterwards. There's not a single calorie in sight!

Is It Time to Manage Your Stress and Stop Smoking?

Throughout the year there are often several Stop Smoking initiatives. With numbers falling to just under 20% of the adult population smoking in the UK in 2015, there are still an estimated 80,000 smoking-related deaths each year and hundreds of children reportedly take up smoking each week. ASH (Action on Smoking and Health) reports that 2.1 million people now use e-cigarettes, all of whom are current or ex-smokers. Support to stop smoking is offered by various health providers, hoping to motivate smokers into deciding to quit.

Here are tips to help you stop smoking when you're ready:

- Join a stop smoking initiative like the 28 day Stoptober campaign, as research in Australia, Canada, UK and the United States shows that smokers who sign up together are far (67%) more likely to quit if their partner also stops smoking and 36% more likely to quit if they stop with a friend. Having a non-smoking partner or circle of friends also increases the likelihood of being a non-smoker.

- Identify the differences between your cigarettes, the various moods and triggers that prompt you to smoke. Some cigarettes will be more important to you than others. Several will be smoked without thinking, out of habit, on auto pilot; perhaps after a phone call, with coffee, after food or when driving. Decide to stop the cigarettes that are smoked automatically without thinking, with no real desire or sense of enjoyment.

- Distractions can help you manage the habitual smoking times. As human beings we can only think of one thing at once, so intercept those vulnerable moments by counting slowly to 100, becoming involved in a conversation, walking to the water cooler for a drink or reading something interesting. The urge for a cigarette often then subsides.

- Change your routine and do things in a different order, thus removing the automatic association with smoking. Use a different mug for your brew, travel another route to work, maybe even rearrange your furniture so you don't unthinkingly sit and reach for a cigarette. Ensure that your home, car and clothes are fresh so that there's no smell of cigarettes in close proximity to you.

- Consider what cigarettes mean to you. Are they a treat, a secret pleasure, a reward or a way to manage stress, frustration, anger? Find better, more appropriate ways to introduce some quality 'me' time into your life. A relaxing bath, a walk with friends, going for a run or listening to music can be much nicer alternatives.

- If you were going for a smoke and at that very moment received an important call from a client or family member, you would probably instantly forget about the cigarette and take the call. Appreciate how easily you can be distracted. Take control back and focus on changing the mind-set that has supported your habit.

- Money is rarely the reason that people stop smoking. Even so, it's a consideration. Save the money you would have spent on cigarettes in a big glass jar and watch it accumulate. Use it to do something special. Maybe buy something lovely for yourself or your home, or treat family and friends to a fun trip or outing.

Enjoy the rewards as you find better ways to spend your hard-earned money.

- Hypnotherapy is widely recognised as an effective way to reinforce a smoker's determination to quit and become a non-smoker. Many people started smoking when they were quite young, perhaps because of peer pressure or a lack of confidence. Hypnotherapy can help release you from the burden of your old, unwanted habit, whilst improving your confidence, self-esteem and helping you find better, more effective ways to deal with stress and difficult times in your life.

If you decide to stop smoking as part of a national initiative or commit to a New Year's Resolution it's good to use it as an opportunity to be part of a shared commitment, hopefully supporting others in your joint endeavour. Almost immediate benefits are reduced blood pressure, easier breathing and better circulation, as well as more spare cash and the removal of the social limitations of being a smoker.

As you become fitter, healthier and more focussed on a better quality of life why not regard this as the start of a positive new you, where you really begin to look after yourself and make better choices about your daily life. A healthier diet, a little exercise and the decision to take good care of yourself can really improve many areas of your life, both physically and mentally.

The Thing About Drinking

Many places have a strong culture around drinking alcohol, especially in relation to social and relaxation activities. Drinking is often seen as an essential part of a good night out.

It's not that long ago that people would be asked if they wanted 'one for the road', in reference to having another drink before they left to drive home. Many business events included lunches where wine and liqueurs were liberally dispensed.

Most people are now more committed to being fit and healthy, and are aware of the consequences that an overindulgence of alcohol can have on their health, safety and work performance. Many businesses have got rid of the bar in the management suite and now offer working lunches with sandwiches and soft drinks.

But alcohol still plays an important part in many people's psyche as a way to relax, manage stress and have a good time.

- Young people often feel that it's normal to drink heavily, sometimes even before leaving home for an evening out. Downing shots and binge drinking are seen as fairly commonplace. Parents can be torn between letting their children 'have fun', or being seen as an overbearing dictator.

  Notice if their drinking is to do with peer pressure, stress, confidence-related issues or simply a phase that they're going through, a part of growing up. As a parent it can be important to keep channels of communication open so that you can monitor any areas of concern in your children's lives.

- Young professionals live high-pressured lives, where they work hard with many career-driven demands and then want to play hard, have fun and enjoy a great social life. The desire to do both fully can mean that alcohol is used as a fast way to deal with the stress of their busy lives and access instant relaxation after a heavy day at the office. I know that often my busy, stressed clients say they pour themselves a large drink when they walk through their front door, even before they've taken their coats off. They regard it as a way of signalling the end of their working day.

- Older people may have different stresses in their lives. Personal relationships may be fraught or have ended. They may be lonely and single, or their career and business hopes and dreams may not have worked out as they would have liked. Alcohol may be a reliable companion or it's used to dull out the disappointments and hurts of the outside world. Just pouring a drink each evening can introduce a sense of comfort and well-being.

But drinking can creep up on us and become a threat to our health and happiness. An occasional glass can become a more regular occurrence, which gradually increases in volume over time. And don't forget that home measures often have very little resemblance to the standard measures in a pub or bar! With approximately 635 calories in a bottle of wine there are also the weight implications to consider too!

Here are a few tips to help, if you feel the need to cut back on your intake:

- Designate some alcohol-free evenings in the week. Some people decide not to drink on week nights and then cut back a little at weekends.

- Buy some beautiful, quality glasses, smaller than you normally use. Enjoy using them, making the times you drink a more sensory experience. Appreciate the look and feel of the glass and savour how much better your drink tastes.

- Buy good quality wine and make drinking a more mindful experience as you give your full attention to the aroma, flavour and colour of your drink.

- Put the glass down between sips, and take your time over each mouthful.

- Wait until your glass is empty before allowing it to be re-filled. That way you can monitor how much you've had to drink. Waiters are often quick to top up each customer's glass. They're keen to sell another bottle!

- Think of alcohol-free ways to have fun:

  - ➤ Team sports can provide fun, competition, exercise and friendly rivalry.
  - ➤ Theatre or cinema trips, dance classes or ten-pin bowling can all be enjoyable and satisfying alcohol-free nights out.
  - ➤ Go for a long walk, followed by a supper party where you enjoy a casserole that has been cooking all day in the slow cooker, a great way to share relaxation with family and friends.
  - ➤ As a single person, think of non-alcoholic treats; a long leisurely bath, your favourite book, sipping a mug of hot chocolate or an early night with a favourite film.

Being a regular drinker can gradually increase into heavy drinking or drink dependency if we don't remain aware of what we're doing. Learn to manage your drinking and your ability to take it or leave it. Keep control whilst enjoying a drink. Appreciate an occasional glass or two of wine as one of the pleasures in life.

How to Get the Most Out of Your Exercise and Manage Stress

Exercise should be an important part of our lives for a myriad of reasons, from maintaining good health to managing stress. For many people keep fit and exercise may seem reminiscent of school days and being stood nervously waiting to be picked for a team, or being made to run miles across cold, muddy fields. Let's consider how to change that viewpoint into something more fun and viable which can add enjoyment and value to our lives.

- Many people do like the commitment of joining a gym. They pay their annual membership fee and that in itself motivates them to get their money's worth. By adding it to their regular routine they attend automatically. They may find they enjoy the social interaction when they go, meeting the same people when they attend regularly. Gyms frequently offer different activities under the one roof, swimming, exercise classes and equipment as well as specialist classes like martial arts, yoga and over 50s sessions. Many provide a crèche too. There's usually access to many facilities by being a member of a gym.

- Think outside the box for ways to exercise. You could get off the bus a stop early, or leave home a little sooner in order to walk instead of drive. Use the stairs instead of the lift, or go for a stroll at lunchtime instead of sitting in the office. There are many positive ways to change your old routine, have some 'me' time and learn to manage stress.

- Do things that you enjoy. There's no point planning to do exercise that you don't enjoy. The least opportunity would then provide a reason to stop doing it. Find something that sounds enjoyable and fun. That way you will be more likely to stick with it.

- Exercise with friends. Arranging to exercise together can be a good way of turning exercise into a sociable, fun use of your time. It's a good way of motivating each other to stay with your commitment. The problem with exercising as a group though can be that if one or two fall by the wayside it can discourage the rest of the group. Pick people who are likely to stick with the plan!

- Exercise with your partner. Sharing an interest can enhance your relationship and provide an opportunity to talk whilst enjoying some quality time together. You could discover interesting walks, learn to play golf or tennis or share a bike ride. This time could provide a valuable alternative to watching TV or spending time pursuing separate interests elsewhere.

- Vary the routine. Some people find gym workouts boring. Look for variety or unusual things to do that stimulate or bring a challenge to your life. Make it fun. Go dancing, take up a new sport or go for a game of ten-pin bowling.

- Some people prefer to participate in outdoor activities over the summer months, so look for tennis lessons, horse riding, walking groups and hill climbing. Even bird-watching and nature trails provide opportunities to exercise and can be shared with your children as a family activity.

   Fresh air, nature and exercise are a good combination and are an effective way of keeping in touch with the outdoors whilst managing stress at the same time.

- Set a challenge. Some people thrive on having a goal to work towards. It keeps them motivated. There may be a local charity event or the opportunity to be sponsored to raise charity money as a private effort amongst your group, or a personal goal to lose weight. Whatever works for you is good.

- Get a personal trainer. This is a way of having an exercise routine personally tailored to you, your abilities and fitness level, with your goals in mind. A trainer will keep you on track and vary the routine so that you do different things that keep your body challenged and working to improve.

- Eat well. When you are exercising it is important to drink plenty of fluids, eat well, feed your muscles and stay healthy. This is the best way to get fit, toned and positive. It's also an important and viable way of managing stress too.

CHAPTER EIGHT

Stress and Final Thoughts

This book has covered many key areas of life, hopefully providing you with plenty of tips that can be incorporated into your day-to-day living. Its aim has been to introduce you to different ways of looking at things, as well as helping you review some of the choices that arise when dealing with stressful situations.

This chapter includes a mini-recap, as well as some stress management tools that may be of interest.

Why not Make Our Own Good Fortune?

Some people feel certain that they were born unlucky, they never catch a break. They struggle with their health, relationships and never seem to have any money, success or good fortune however hard they work. These people may well feel that they were born unlucky or even suspect that karma from a previous life is ruining any chance of happiness they may ever hope to have.

Then there are those people who always seem to land on their feet, whatever happens. They appear to live a charmed existence, everything they do turns to gold, success and good fortune.

Some may be born with serious handicaps or impediments to success and yet achieve fantastic goals whilst others born into a gilded existence with good looks, fortune and intelligence may end up with a disastrous life. There are times when some of us are prompted to ask, 'Was I born unlucky or is luck an attitude of mind?'

Some people are certain that 'luck' is an attitude of mind, that the way they think, feel and behave is instrumental in attracting either good or bad fortune their way. There are those who are great at seeing the potential in every setback and refuse to give up. But lifestyle, opportunities and circumstances can significantly influence our chances of success.

However there are certain factors that can help us manage situations in a more positive way.

- **Perspective** is an important factor in how we deal with misfortune and setbacks. Some people may simply shrug their shoulders and say 'that's life'. Others may become devastated and inconsolable when things go wrong or not to plan. These people may take knockbacks personally and feel that nothing good ever happens to them and that they constantly attract bad luck. They become so focussed on every omission, rejection and hurt that they fail to notice the many good things that happen to them each day.

- **Setbacks, mistakes and knocks** provide great ways to develop new skills, interact with others, ask for advice and learn to think outside the box. Many people say that their 'bad luck' brought them some of the best learning experiences they ever had, the ones they never forgot.

Redundancy is often a devastating and life-changing experience and yet, years later people are often heard to say that being made redundant was the best thing that ever happened to them. It forced them into a new direction, one they are often later thankful for but would never have had the nerve to try without a push.

- **Rejection** should not be taken personally or regarded as bad luck. If we decline a waiter's recommendation in a restaurant we don't expect him to burst into tears, and yet many of us become distressed or offended if our ideas or suggestions are rejected. If someone doesn't agree with what we say, rejects our idea or discards our opinion it shouldn't be regarded as a personal affront. Becoming stronger and better able to cope with feedback is an important life skill. Hypnotherapy can support us to become more resilient, to treat these situations more philosophically, so learning and treating setbacks more constructively.

- **Managing a positive balance** in life means ensuring there are some areas where we can guarantee positive feedback. If work is a challenge and feels constantly stressful and draining then we need to spend time on developing good relationships, hobbies, interests and activities that provide plenty of positive recognition. When we spend time doing things that we're good at, with people who care about us, we ensure that we receive praise, recognition and good attention.

- **Don't put all your eggs in one basket**. By having friends, interests and activities in a few different areas we diversify, spread the load and maximise our potential for success into several areas. That way, if one area doesn't work out too well or causes problems for us, we can move on or reduce its impact by focussing on other, more positive areas.

By staying focussed and keeping control of our choices we're better able to provide balance, positive outlook and a sense of optimism. Then bad luck becomes less noticeable, is dealt with speedily and its impact is minimised. We're able to notice the 'good luck' more readily. Or as the world-class professional golfer Jack Nicklaus used to say, 'the more I practice, the luckier I get'. Working hard, having the right attitude and learning from mistakes supports you in achieving what you want to achieve in life.

Manage Stress with Effective Stress Management Techniques

Some stress is an important part of everyday life. It helps us react to situations better, perform with a heightened level of awareness and achieve a more focussed way of thinking. But living in a permanent state of stress is counter-productive, draining and bad for our long-term health.

Let's look at some useful ways to manage stress:

- **Learning to prioritise** is an important technique in managing stress. We can become habituated to instantly reacting whenever there is a request for work or help, but learning to prioritise is an important way to manage the many demands on our time and attention.

- **Seeing things through** from start to finish is important, as it can be tempting when stressed to start one piece of work, then another and have several projects on the go at once. Apply this rule equally at home or at work. By drifting from one job to the next, but completing none can leave a feeling of dissatisfaction at the end of the day. If a work task has to be left part way through make sure that you make clear notes so that it can be resumed quickly upon your return, without having to retrace your steps first.

- **Delegate**. Let others help and take a pride in being given some responsibility. They may become more proficient, experienced and may even offer useful ideas and suggestions as a consequence.

It can take a little time and patience to teach someone new skills, but in the long-term it usually pays off.

- **Say 'no' sometimes.** This is a useful way to manage stress for several reasons. It makes other people appreciate that you're busy, gives you a reminder that you have some control over the way you allocate your time and allows you to focus on doing what you're already doing with a clear, calm mind.

- **Practice self-hypnosis.** It need only take a second or two to mentally visit a calm place in nature, like a garden, beach or waterfall, and enjoy the sense of peace it brings, or to practice telling yourself some positive affirmations and statements. Use these as effective ways to manage stress, boost your confidence and improve your self-esteem. Self-hypnosis can act as a quick mini-break at times of pressure, when you're perhaps in need of time to de-clutter your thinking and access calm, peace and clear thinking.

- **Self-hypnosis** can also provide a fast and effective way to draw a line between work and home. Some people find it hard to switch off at the end of the day. They find themselves constantly checking their phone or emails, unable to stop worrying or stressing about their latest project or task. Practice breathing techniques and self-hypnosis as an effective way of letting go of invasive thoughts and setting better habits in place.

Remind yourself to value the other areas of your life, your family, friends, hobbies and interests as well as work. By introducing stress management techniques it becomes easier to find a balance between all those different areas. You establish a better quality of life and establish a healthy work/life balance that brings satisfaction, pleasure as well as challenge and only occasional stress.

Writing as an Aid to Coping with Stress

In these fast-paced times actually sitting to write a card, a letter or keep a journal can seem like an old-fashioned notion, too far out of our thought processes to actually entertain. But writing things down can be a satisfying and effective way of clarifying our thoughts, clearing our mind and working things out.

The Importance of Keeping a Journal

A journal is an excellent mechanism for expressing our thoughts and feelings, the very things that we may struggle to say out loud. Writing about our distress, the mixed emotions and unsettling thoughts and feelings that we may be going through, can help to gradually resolve matters, so that life can continue in a more positive way. It's a means of externalising things and putting them into a better order or perspective.

Once we've finished with an entry we can close the book, safe in the knowledge that those personal insights are contained in a safe place; they are now being processed, and need no longer occupy all that space inside our heads.

At times when we're feeling lonely or trying to deal with a problem that we feel we cannot share, keeping a journal can be an important refuge, providing solace and comfort. It can be a valuable way to express ourselves, to work through and hopefully come to a better understanding about things.

Re-reading these entries at a later date can be helpful too, as it allows us to reflect on how far we've come. We can read and notice how various insights and changes have evolved over the period of writing.

This is why it's useful to regularly update your journal. It helps you begin to make sense of why things happen; why you perhaps continue to behave and react in the way you do. It helps you gain insight into your thought processes and the underlying reasons behind your actions. Also, it provides an interesting document, charting your progress and journey to a better place.

Many people support their therapy sessions by keeping a journal. Often issues that are discussed during a session are reflected on or even dreamt about afterwards. Using a journal can allow the therapeutic process to continue, through the writing down of feelings, remembering and making sense of experiences and documenting the impact they have had in your life.

Gratitude can feature in your journal. Write down the things that you're grateful for in your life. You may be unsure where to start, but gradually it can become easier. Think of the special people, the times and experiences that have contributed to you being the person you are today. Give thanks for them and the valuable lessons along the way. Even tough experiences can sometimes be acknowledged for providing significant opportunities for personal development.

A Happy Book is a mini journal, used to capture entries every day, ones that would have been unlikely to be remembered. Treasured little vignettes can be regularly noted, dated and stored, able to be revisited, especially if feeling a little down or low. A lovely sight in nature, an act of kindness or an achievement can all be held forever in your special book, there to be dipped into whenever wanted or needed. And a Happy Book is a good way to remind yourself that good things do happen in your life.

Privacy is often an important reason to keep a journal. There may be concerns that some of our actions, thoughts or feelings may be judged in a negative way and we may not wish to disclose those parts of ourselves to others. When we're feeling vulnerable it's good to have a safe place, like a journal, where we can express ourselves and allow those feelings to become more manageable.

So, keep your journal in a private place. Even the closest relationships often draw the line at sharing their journal. It's the place where momentary, fleeting doubts, fears and concerns are expressed and worked through and so, is often regarded as a work-in-progress.

Write a Letter to Explain How You Feel

When a relationship goes wrong it may result in both parties feeling unable to properly communicate how they feel. They may have no idea why things have turned out so badly or they may be unsure as to what they want to have happen next. When this situation occurs there are often several things that we want to say or explain, but finding the best time, way or the right opportunity to do this may be too stressful to even think about.

Sometimes a relationship counsellor or mediator may be able to help. When both parties agree to this, it can be a good way to open up communications and understanding. Other times, one person deciding to write a letter to the other can bring about change and help to improve mutual understanding.

Writing a letter can be a good way to help improve empathy and understanding in a relationship.

The advantage of letter writing is that the writer can take their time to collect their thoughts, consider what they need to say and then finally put it down on paper. This exercise alone can help a person to clarify how they feel about their relationship.

Many people find they become entrenched in arguments when they are involved in face to face discussions. One person may be more vocal. They are perhaps perceived as intelligent, good at putting together the perfect, irrefutable argument or as someone who's not prepared to listen to another point of view. The other may dislike confrontation or perhaps feels that they won't be listened to anyway. A letter can be a way of by-passing those constraints, composing one's thoughts and feelings and laying them out to be expressed without interruption. It can be a successful way for both people to have their say.

It can be useful to write the first draft of your letter and then put it away for a few days, to be revisited later. It's often interesting to reread it after a day or two, then make corrections and phrase things differently, if it's felt appropriate. Let writing your letter take as long as is necessary until you feel confident enough to send it to its intended recipient.

A letter provides an opportunity to explain oneself, with no interruptions or arguments to stop the flow. The reader can keep it to read where and whenever is convenient and as often as they want. It provides an opportunity for the writer to outline their viewpoint, hopes, regrets and possibly desired outcome from the situation. And the reader is then able to take their time to consider what's been said and mull over their response.

Some people may use letter writing purely for their own benefit, as a way to work through unresolved issues with someone who has caused them serious pain, but who is no longer around. There may be unfinished business which causes them distress and which needs addressing. Or there may be issues of bullying, abuse or harm which they prefer not to deal with face to face.

They may take their time to ensure that it's well written and covers everything they need to say, but they may then choose not to send the finished letter. They may decide to symbolically burn it, bury it or even throw it out to sea. Whatever helps them feel that they've dealt with the matter fully and are now able to live free from its influence. It can be very cathartic to write a letter to clear the air and is a useful way of avoiding the confrontation that may well arise with a face-to-face meeting or a telephone call.

Letter writing may be regarded as an out-dated mode of communication, but it's still valuable as a way of explaining our point of view and expressing ourselves and our personal feelings. Writing a letter to explain how we feel about something demonstrates that the matter is important to us and that we have given it some serious consideration.

A letter is also an important way to send recognition, appreciation and that someone's been remembered and is in our thoughts. There's often a feel good factor attached to receiving a letter. Some people tend to only receive bills and junk mail through the door, so a card or thoughtful letter can be gratefully received. To some extent, email has brought back the art of keeping in touch through the written word, but to many people a handwritten letter or a card seems rather more genuine and sincere.

Clear Your Mind by Using a List

Some people use their journal to write lists. It can be a useful place to record the things that you want to do in life, the goals, dreams and things that would make a difference to you and to your life. By committing them to paper they become more concrete and may even start to take shape as serious options, worthy of consideration. Lists can take the pressure off and make life appear easier and more manageable.

Lists can be used for many different purposes:

- **Worry list.** My husband was a big fan of worry lists. He would recommend that his clients took the time to put all their worries, fears and concerns down on paper. It sometimes took a considerable amount of time to do this as new things would frequently crop up which needed to be added. He would suggest that they continued writing until they felt that everything was down on paper.

Then, the list should be kept somewhere private, safe and secure. Whenever a new worry arose it could be added to the list and whenever something was resolved it could be crossed off. By having them on paper a person could feel reassured that they were not going to forget any of those items and could keep their mind clear to work on each matter in hand.

- **Business lists**. I've known successful business people who kept everything in their heads and prided themselves on never writing anything down. But it's a stressful way to live. Lists are an effective way of knowing that our major tasks for the day have been identified, are written down and can be easily referred to. Either last thing at night or at the beginning of each day we can refer to it for an overview. A list provides a way to clearly focus the mind.

- **Check lists**. It's useful to go through a list and prioritise each item. Essential items can then be ranked in order. Obviously if new, urgent items occur throughout the day they can be added and the list can be reordered, but a list gives a greater sense of control and provides a reference point for what needs doing at a glance.

- **Daily lists**. Some people feel dissatisfied that they achieve nothing or very little each day. Writing down the day's anticipated tasks can provide motivation and discipline. Then crossing off what has been done can be a satisfying exercise. It can be surprising to note how many new, unlisted, unexpected things occur each day and it can be valuable to reflect on how we use our time. Is it productive to do these extra things? Many people achieve far more than they give themselves credit for each day.

- **Food lists** can be an effective way to monitor our eating habits. Personal trainers often suggest food diaries or lists so that we can itemise what we actually eat in a day. Many sneaky treats are often forgotten about over the course of a day. Writing down every biscuit and snack can make for a shock at the end of a day or week.

- **Lists** can also be a valuable way of keeping control of things that happen only occasionally. Some people still use Christmas card lists. That way they can check from one year to the next that they have not forgotten anyone. Also lists of gifts given and received can be a good way to manage present giving.

The Best Affirmations

We all talk to ourselves constantly, that internal chatter that happens when we're feeling nervous, uneasy or unsure of ourselves. It's probably quite rare for many of us to tell ourselves, 'well done' or 'great job'. However there will be important times when we will really focus and tell ourselves, 'you can do it', but most times that inner dialogue will have a negative voice.

Positive affirmations are ways of introducing good self-talk into those areas where it is most needed. Many people have issues with their confidence, so it can be useful to reflect on the areas where confidence is a struggle. Some people may feel vulnerable in a work situation, especially in situations where the people around them appear to be exceptionally professional, experienced and capable. For others it may be social situations, where their friends appear attractive, smart and relaxed.

They may feel awkward, shy or unsure as to what to say or do in those situations. Some may have been told as children that they should be seen and not heard, told off for asking too many questions, or been chastised for being over exuberant. Hearing negative messages about ourselves can, over time, cause us to become unsure of our behaviour.

Affirmations are about the way we talk to ourselves. We may come to realise that we talk to ourselves negatively, and as such reinforce low expectations and self-belief. We may have positive affirmations suggested to us by others but find that they sit uncomfortably with us.

Selecting the most appropriate affirmations for ourselves and our lifestyles is an important step to take.

The important thing about affirmations is that they have to sit well with the person who is saying them. Affirmations need to be phrased in the present tense and resonate well when they are being said. So an affirmation is not about negating another person and their importance. It is more about acknowledging that if we are well and happy then the other people in our lives benefit and get the best from us. We become more positive and satisfied in our roles.

Affirmations about our body:

Many people struggle with the way they feel about their body. Women may feel especially self-conscious, particularly after childbirth. Men may look at other men and compare themselves negatively; their muscle tone, height, physique and looks. Learning to like ourselves and our imperfections can be a tough exercise. Appreciating that our body is a testament to who we are and what we've been through is important.

Childbirth, surgery, stress and health concerns all take their toll on our bodies. Affirmations that include the phrase 'I am learning to like myself', or 'I am becoming more accepting of myself and my body' can acknowledge that we are moving towards being more positive and are starting to feel better about ourselves.

Affirmations within the family:

Many men and women juggle several roles and often feel guilty about neglecting their family because of the compromises that they have to make to support the demands on their time and energy. Sometimes there's a need to delegate and let others shoulder some responsibility, but that can cause feelings of guilt to occur.

Letting others down or feeling inadequate can sometimes happen if family, friends or paid help are called upon, or if priorities dictate that an unpopular decision has to be taken. Affirmations which acknowledge that it is a positive step to allow others to help can start to change that perspective. Statements like 'I do what I do out of love', 'I am doing my best and my best let's others help too' can be effective, but they work best when you choose the words and have found the best phrase to suit you.

Affirmations at work:

Women are often all too aware of the difficulties of balancing the demands of home and work. They are conscious that many work environments require women to be especially competent and this means that there is often a struggle to do more, achieve more and continuously prove how committed they are.

Men can feel torn between being a good provider and working hard in their career or business and also being available to participate in home and family life.

Affirmations for work can include taking the pressure off, relieving stress and allowing enough to be sufficient. Affirmations like 'I am enough. What I do is enough.' said regularly and with feeling can help to ease the stress of the situation.

Becoming aware of the role that positive self-talk plays in shaping our mind-set and self-esteem can enable better confidence and a more helpful outlook to occur. Positive affirmations can enable both men and women to view themselves and their role with a more healthy perspective. Being kinder in the way we talk to ourselves is an important step in managing stress.

ABOUT THE AUTHOR

As a highly respected counsellor and hypnotherapist, Susan has been helping people to transform their lives for many years. She set up Lifestyle Therapy Counselling and Hypnotherapy with her late husband and her practice is based in Altrincham, South Manchester.

Susan works with individuals, helping them to cope better with stress and the pressures of daily life; with couples to provide relationship counselling and improve communications; and in business to provide support to management, staff members and teams. She is also a highly regarded hypnotherapy trainer and public speaker.

Susan is a regular contributor to national and local BBC radio stations, including BBC Radio 5 Live and has appeared on BBC Breakfast. She also writes regularly for many local, national and international websites and publications including The Huffington Post, as well as several business, women's and fitness magazines.

Prior to working as a counsellor and hypnotherapist, Susan worked for many years with a blue chip company and has experienced the stresses of balancing a corporate and personal life.

Susan qualified with the Academy of Curative Hypnotherapy, holds the Counselling Advanced Level 4 Diploma, is an accredited member of the Stress Management Society, Member of the Hypnotherapy Association and a Member of the National Council for Hypnotherapy (Accredited). She is registered with the Complementary and Natural Healthcare Council (CNHC) and is a member of the College of Medicine.

CONTACT SUSAN

Visit her websites: www.susanleigh.net and www.lifestyletherapy.net

Email   Susan at susan@susanleigh.net

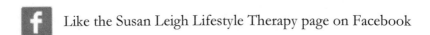 Like the Susan Leigh Lifestyle Therapy page on Facebook

 Follow Susan on Twitter @SusanLeigh1